Can You
BEAT THE
BEAST?

MARK LABBETT

Can You
BEAT THE
BEAST?

HAVE YOU GOT WHAT IT TAKES
TO CHALLENGE THE BEAST?

First published in Great Britain in 2022 by Cassell, an imprint of
Octopus Publishing Group Ltd
Carmelite House
50 Victoria Embankment
London EC4Y 0DZ
www.octopusbooks.co.uk

An Hachette UK Company
www.hachette.co.uk

Distributed in the US by
Hachette Book Group
1290 Avenue of the Americas
4th and 5th Floors
New York, NY 10104

Distributed in Canada by
Canadian Manda Group
664 Annette St.
Toronto, Ontario, Canada M6S 2C8

ISBN 978-1-78840-353-5

A CIP catalogue record for this book is available from the British Library.

Printed and bound in Great Britain

10 9 8 7 6 5 4 3 2 1

Text written by Christian Guiltenane
Quiz questions supplied by Redtooth Quizzes (www.redtoothquiz.co.uk)

Publisher: Trevor Davies
Senior Editor: Alex Stetter
Designer: Jeremy Tilston
Senior Production Controller: Allison Gonsalves

CONTENTS

INTRODUCTION

Welcome to this very special quiz book. Are you sitting comfortably? Are you ready to get those little grey cells of yours bouncing around in your head? Good! But before you do, I think it's only polite for us to get better acquainted.

I probably don't need to introduce myself. After all, why else would you have bought this rather fine book if it wasn't to find out more about ME? But if, on the off chance you picked it up because you were rather taken by the dashing chap on the cover or merely have an interest in becoming a better quizzer, let me introduce myself properly.

My name is Mark 'The Beast' Labbett, superbrain quizzer and one of the stars of ITV's hugely successful daytime quiz show, *The Chase*. You know the one – the glossy, shiny game show that's shown every weekday at teatime (and the occasional weekend) and presented by funnyman and actor Bradley Walsh. Each episode, I or one of the other five Chasers – Anne 'The Governess' Hegerty, Paul 'The Sinnerman' Sinha, Jenny 'The Vixen' Ryan, Shaun 'The Dark Destroyer' Wallace and Darragh 'The Menace' Ennis – take turns to compete against four ordinary folks like you who are delusional enough to think they can beat us.

They rarely do.

As you know from my appearances on *The Chase*, I am no shrinking violet when it comes to my self-belief. When I walk out on that set to face a trembling contestant, I'm there to win. And in most cases I do, depending on how fast and efficiently they get through the questions with Bradley. You could call me arrogant. In fact, many have. And you know what? Even I think it. Yes, I'm arrogant and egotistical. That's why you love me, right? But unlike so many arrogant so-and-sos in the public eye, I can back it up as I know what I'm good at.

You see, I am officially a genius. But only just. In 2019, while filming spin-off show *The Chasers Road Trip* for ITV, my IQ was measured at 151 and I scored well into the top 1 per cent in mental calculations, neural processing speed and memory recall.

I've been lucky over the years that I've been good with numbers and retaining information, all of which came in handy when I was studying at university and working as a teacher. It was also a godsend when I fell in love with quizzing and it helped me build a healthy reputation among the quiz community and eventually led me to pursue a wildly successful global TV career in later life.

Is the knack of remembering facts and figures a God-given natural talent? Or is it a skill that can be practised and developed? I think it's a bit of both. I most definitely think some people are inclined to be interested in the world around them and soak up information. However, I also think there are ways in which we can help ourselves take in information and remember it. In this book, I will share many of my quizzing adventures and offer handy hints on how you can become a better quizzer. I will even give you some insight into what I think producers are looking for when it comes to hunting down new Chasers!

But the best part of this book is that you'll find general knowledge quizzes and a handful of specialist subjects for you to test your quizzing skills and to find out if you can outsmart me, The Beast.

I have already completed the quizzes – honestly, I might add! – so once you've worked your way through them yourself (no cheating now), we can determine if, as I highly suspect, I have whupped your ass, or if, by some bizarre twist of fate, you have beaten me.

EARLY DAYS

Right, let's get started. I was born in Tiverton in Devon in 1965. I was so eager to get into the world that I was born around four weeks premature, weighing in at a decidedly average 7lb. If I'd gone full term, I reckon I would have been a fairly big unit. One of my younger brothers, however, trumped me. Born almost three years after me (and twenty months after our middle brother Paul), Big Phil officially weighed in at 10lb 8oz. He was such a whopper that the exhausted midwife said: 'That's the biggest effing baby I've ever seen.' After Phil's painful arrival, Mum and Dad unsurprisingly decided to call it quits at three kids.

Of course, our size shouldn't have come as a surprise to Mum and Dad as height runs in our family. Dad was 6 foot 4, while Mum was 5 foot 10. When my brothers and I were kids, a doctor predicted that we'd grow up to be very, very tall and said we'd most likely reach 6 foot 5, 6 foot 6 and 6 foot 8. He was right. I'm 6 foot 6½, Paul's 6 foot 5 and Phil is 6 foot 8.

My mother's family were originally from Manchester but my father's were all Devonian and were either muck spreaders or policemen. In fact, for many generations, a career in the police force was inevitable. However, my dad, John, who went to Acton County Grammar School, chose not to join the police. Disappointing A-level results meant that university wasn't on the cards so he embarked instead on three years of military service with the RAF. After that he joined the civil service as a meat inspector and livestock officer and pretty much spent his entire career there, ending up at the local abattoir in Salisbury.

Not the most glamorous of career paths, I'll admit, but it was one that had its benefits. Workers were able to purchase quality meat at wholesale prices, which meant our freezer at home was nearly always full of prime protein. It might have been the reason Phil, Paul and I grew up to be as big as we are. Because meat was such a big part of our lives, we as a family soon learned about basic butchering. I had no qualms about it, I wasn't squeamish. If you handed me a leg of lamb or a quarter of beef, I'd have it butchered up in no time and neatly stored away in the chest freezer, where we'd live off it for most of the winter. In spite of my enthusiasm for chopping up meat for our dinner table, I never had any aspirations to follow in my father's footsteps. Nor did I learn any skills that would set me up for the future – though I guess you could argue I do have a habit of occasionally butchering the quizzers' chances of taking home any money on *The Chase*.

We lived a comfortable life in Salisbury. We were what you would describe as a lower-middle-class family. We did okay but we were never wealthy. We didn't go on a foreign holiday until I was 16 – a chaotic car trip to the middle of France. It might not sound like an exciting adventure, but imagine the five of us – who, remember, were all pretty large at the time – tightly packed into a Peugeot. Not exactly what you might call fun. And by the time we got there, it was our poor old Peugeot that had suffered the most and was a gasping, rickety mess.

We lived in a nice big house that was designed to accommodate the larger individual. When we had our kitchen extension built, we ensured that all the cupboards were set up a little bit higher than normal. Some builders would have baulked, saying we should think about who we might sell the house on to one day. But needs must and we built huge deep cupboards that stretched all the way up to the ceiling. As it turned out, selling the place wasn't a problem, because the people who bought it from us were tall themselves, so the special features we'd added to the place were actually its selling points.

By the time my brothers and I started school, my parents had made sure we could read and write. We were also constantly tested on our times tables, which I excelled at – although I once proudly stated that 2x2x2 was 6, my only arithmetic mistake in primary school. (The answer's 8, in case you were confused by that.)

At school, it was clear that I was more adept with numbers than with the written word. In my Year Three examinations, I finished first in maths and twenty-ninth in English. It was then that my massive ego got a hefty kickstart. By Year Five I was second in maths and eighth in English. I was pretty chuffed and wasn't shy about letting others know about it. At that age you don't really have any self-awareness or understand that some people find academic subjects much tougher. It also perhaps gives an insight into my developing brain and personality that I can recall all of those things from memory.

Salisbury at the time had two academic systems. One half of the city had a selective educational system, separated into single-sex schools. The other half was full of co-educational comprehensives. Mum and Dad knew we were brighter than most from the reports they'd had from our teachers at school, and so they were encouraged to get us the best secondary education possible. As luck would have it, Dad accepted a promotion at work which meant that we moved to the catchment area for the boys' grammar school.

Phil, Paul and I were all fortunate enough to pass the Eleven Plus and attend Bishop Wordsworth's School, the local boys' grammar. In effect we got one of the best educations money didn't buy. Academically life was rather easy and, with a science-based curriculum, I would go on to gain five A-levels and ten O-levels. However, I was socially inept and never really had a big friendship group. That's just the way I was wired. If you asked me to name someone from school, I couldn't – I'm not in contact with anybody from grammar school. Some people wonder if I'm on the spectrum – I'm not sure, I'm just happy doing my own thing. Always have been.

Don't get me wrong. My childhood wasn't unpleasant, I wasn't lonely. I just wasn't the kind of person who had a big group of friends. However, there was a period of time when I was around 13 or 14 when I was bullied by other boys because I was smaller than them. Quite a few of them looked like fully grown men, towering above me at 5 foot 11 or 6 foot, while I was just 5 foot 9. It wasn't until I was 16 that I suddenly shot up to 6 foot and kept growing.

In fairness, I don't think my ego helped me make friends either. I found learning things at school easy and was always surprised when the other lads didn't. I'd ask them why they spent so much of their time revising and they'd tell me that they needed to keep reading over stuff so they could take it all in. I was astonished and I couldn't get my head around it because all I had to do was read something once and I remembered it straight away. I genuinely didn't understand why the rest of the boys weren't like me. I mean, in class I was one of those kids who whizzed through my work and grudgingly waited for everyone else to catch up. I don't think I appreciated at the time that we are all wired differently and I made it clear that I was a cut above everyone else. As you can imagine, this air of arrogance didn't exactly help me win too many mates and to this day I have to admit I'm still not great at forging friendships. My saving grace now is the job I do is the ultimate icebreaker. People want to come up and chat to me.

However, it was at school where my interest in quizzing was first sparked. Growing up in the 1970s, my family had always been glued to TV shows like *University Challenge* and *Mastermind* and I'd have no trouble at all answering the questions before the contestants did on screen. It was a gift that was noticed by my history teacher, Mr Shirley, who hosted a general knowledge quiz before we broke up for the summer break. One year, the team I was on won 11–9, thanks to my speed and knowledge. So impressed was Mr Shirley by my sterling performance that he took me to one side and said: 'You know stuff, don't you?' Buoyed by his glowing praise, I was put on a school team and entered into Schools Challenge, a national general knowledge competition founded by Colin Galloway in 1978 that was basically like a schools' version of *University Challenge*. We entered every year and on one occasion my team actually made it to the national quarter-finals. Sadly, we lost out to King Henry VIII School in Abergavenny, a school I would later teach at.

UNI LIFE

As I neared the end of school, I applied to read maths at Exeter College at the University of Oxford. Unsurprisingly, I sailed through the entrance exam, in which I had to complete three papers and solve unusual problems. Because I'd already secured a computer science A-level the year before, I got a conditional offer from Exeter College on the proviso I achieved at least one E grade. This meant I could spend the rest of my summer not fretting as much as my classmates about getting into uni, and instead cheerfully spent my time on the cricket pitch or the athletics track instead. I was pleased that I had been accepted by Exeter, because I was being judged purely on my maths skills rather than my social skills.

That summer I was studying for four A-levels. One, of course, was maths, which I was confident about, as the year before I had scored 88 per cent in a test paper, which I completed in just half an hour. I remember the looks of disdain my schoolmates gave me when I sat back in my chair looking relaxed as they sweated their way through it. But that's the thing – some people are lucky enough to be a natural in a certain area like maths. Others are better with languages.

As I mentioned earlier, I suspect I may be on the spectrum. Many people I know who are on it are good at maths and I think that's because numbers are so easy to deal with. They are based on certain rules. For example, 4x7 is 28. If I ask you again in an hour, 4x7 is still 28 and 7x4 is 28. There is a rule. From my experience of life, people on the spectrum tend to be very good at following rules and don't like it when things get changed, which is probably why they find the logical subjects a bit easier to learn.

In the end I got an A in maths, an A in physics, a B in chemistry and an E in further maths. Yes, an E! Surprised? Well, if I'm honest, I just don't understand algebra as easily as I do numbers.

Although I was happy that my results had helped me breeze into uni, I was still a little disappointed because I'd wanted all As. Who wouldn't? Now I can appreciate that getting an A grade at A-level in the 1970s actually put me in the top 15 per cent of A-level results in the country, which is something of an achievement when you consider that only 3 per cent of the population took A-levels at the time, whereas 60 per cent take them now. So over the years there's been a bit of grade inflation, which makes me feel sorry for kids these days, because if they're not getting straight As in everything then they don't let them in anywhere. But the other problem is, with those top grades easier to come by, kids get buoyed by their success and tend to upgrade their uni choice, only to find out when they get there that they're not quite as good as they thought they were. Academic friends have said to me that an A grade, or certainly A/B grades, is only really necessary if you want to become an academic. Most people don't need a B in maths to work in any kind of graduate profession unless it's in a job that specifically requires maths.

Going to Oxford was certainly a new chapter in my life, not just because it meant I had finally moved away from the family home – it was where I came into close contact with the opposite sex for the first time. That might sound a little dramatic, but don't forget, I was one of three brothers who had spent years at a boys' school, so to suddenly see women was really quite astonishing. I spent my time walking around campus thinking: 'Wow, women – they're a different species.'

It took some getting used to, let me tell you. But don't expect me to furnish you with a variety of saucy tales of romance and debauchery. My love life, sadly, continued to be pretty nonexistent. In fact, I'd say a monk probably got more attention than I did. I'll make no bones about, but I reckon I'm one of those guys who like women but are absolutely useless at being in relationships. And sadly that trend continued for many a year! In fact, I can confidently say that the total amount of time I spent in relationships before I appeared on *The Chase* was probably about 12 months in total. Considering I was 42 when I started on the show, you can imagine how frustrating that must have been for me. I just didn't date and got used to spending a lot of time on my own. In fact, I began to rather enjoy it and I'm not ashamed to admit it. I know lots of people who are comfortably single and I think there's actually something nice about being in a commitment of one – you just do what you want to do. It's all about the way your mind is geared.

So without any romantic adventures to entertain me, I spent a lot of my university years playing sports that benefitted from my 6 foot 6 stature. But I am a low-level sportsman – I'm blessed with a huge frame, which makes me virtually bulletproof, but what I haven't got is fast twitch muscles. If I were to drop down and give you 20 push-ups, it would look like I was doing them in slow motion compared with someone with fast twitch muscles who can go bang, bang, bang and do 3 push-ups to 1 of mine.

Over the three years at college, I played about twenty different sports but was a master of none. I only really got onto the basketball second team – and occasionally the first – because of my height. In fact, the team blatantly told me: 'We can't train height, so you're a shoo-in.' I played centre, which is like being a goalie in football – in other words, I was a big lump who wasn't allowed to shoot, but could jump and catch the ball and more importantly block the other team. So in each game, one of my team-mates would run up the court trying to distract an opposing team player so that they'd blindly crash into me, leaving my team-mate unguarded with a clear shot of the basket. Basically I was a human wall who would leave our opponents being scraped off the ground. I didn't care that my team-mates never passed me the ball – to be honest, I didn't want them to. I was more of a smart sportsman than a talented one.

Away from the sports field I carried on quizzing and took part in the internal quiz competition, representing Exeter's first team. We made it to the semi-final, where we were taken apart by Lady Margaret Hall. Their captain was a chap called Stephen Pearson who these days is better known as 'the Alex Ferguson of *University Challenge*' as he works as a librarian for Manchester University and coaches their quiz teams to success on a regular basis. Also playing for LMH was a young Michael Gove. I will leave it to others to evaluate his political career, but he is possibly one of the most naturally gifted quizzers I have ever seen.

Of course my quizzing ambitions knew no bounds and my big dream was to represent Exeter on *University Challenge*, the show I had grown up watching with my family. However, when I enquired about it, I was told the team had already been picked so I sadly missed out. Instead, a bunch of pals and I went along to support the team at the recording of the show. It wasn't pretty, as Birkbeck College London gave the team their second-worst beating in quizzing history.

I felt sorry for the guys because they really were brilliant academics with first-class honours and doctorates. Their main problem was that they weren't quick enough on the buzzer. After the show, everyone said to me: 'Bloody hell Mark, you'd have got more than them.' And I was like: 'Yeah, I know!' Yep, I was that cocky at just 18, but I knew I had a gift. It sounds odd to say it but I really do believe that I have the job I was born to do. How many people are lucky enough to say that? Even those who don't like me say that I am in the right job and still have the cheek to ask me if can they work alongside me.

In spite of my playing a bunch of team sports, quizzing and working night shifts as a doorman at various bars in the area, Oxford was a strange place and for me felt very isolating. At the start of term, I had the option of sharing a dorm, but chose not to. My only real link to the outside world was via the Royal Mail or the one payphone at the end of the corridor in halls, which you had to book in advance. Now, of course, we can keep in contact with people 24/7 all around the world. But back then, it was so very different. Like school, I didn't really make any lasting friendships at Oxford. That said, when *The Chase* won a BAFTA in 2022, about half a dozen people from college got in touch with me, saying that they'd never have imagined when we graduated in 1986 that I of all people would go on to win a BAFTA.

Eventually it was time to spread my wings and head out into the real world with my pretty mediocre degree and the honour of being University Shot Put Champion of the Year. But I did so with no real idea of what I wanted to do. Eventually, like many before me, I drifted into the great graduate job programme that is teaching. However, while I was waiting to start my PGCE I discovered my future.

In the summer of 1987, I did what I might describe as a gap year, working as a barman at Butlin's in Minehead. It was here that I came across a quiz machine called Give Us a Break, which would ultimately set me on my path to *The Chase*. These machines were modelled on Dave Lee Travis's snooker-based Radio 1 quiz show at the time. For a 20p stake you got up to 18 questions, and if you took the black ball question you would get 75 points and a guaranteed £10. Sounds easy – and it was. Well, for me, at least. The only difficulty was as the game progressed the questions would come at you faster. Luckily, I'm a speed reader and could answer quickly, so I'd triumph every time. It wasn't all plain sailing – some answers I didn't know. There were perhaps 10,000 questions, and to turn wrong answers into right answers I either went to the reference library, teamed up with knowledgeable guests or just plain guessed them. Eventually, these machines became my personal piggy banks, earning me about 200 quid a week, which paid for my nights out.

Every morning or mid-afternoon, I would head down to the bars or the local arcade before my shift and settle down to what I considered the real work of the day.

I was lucky that this very early quiz machine (a) guaranteed a win after 18 questions and (b) never took money away with a wrong answer. The more sophisticated machines of today are far less user-friendly and cost way more to enter. I only play quiz machines for a game or two now – human beings are much easier to beat.

At the end of each week, I'd take a leisurely stroll into Minehead town centre and bank my £200 in pound coins into my account. Eventually, that and a few other machines back in Salisbury would help pay for my first car – a Talbot Solara. To a certain extent, quizzing became a self-financing hobby that paid for my nights out and for pretty much every car ever since then. These days I have graduated mainly to Toyota and Volvo SUVs. Even with the weight loss, I find it difficult to get in and out of many cars, so swanky sports cars are a non-starter for me.

After doing a teacher-training course I taught at various schools from 1989 to 1994. With hindsight, I now know it wasn't right for me, it was a big mistake. I taught maths at the London Oratory School, where I did two years and enjoyed it. I went to Cheltenham College but was made redundant. Then I went to Mill Hill School but didn't think it was for me, as I didn't get on with some of the teachers there. A lot of it was down to me.

Was I a good teacher? I'm not sure. I don't think I was consistent enough. When I was on form and full of energy, I was wonderful. But when I was tired I got bored so easily. That's what frustrates me – I know I could have been a great teacher. But I just wasn't in the right frame of mind. That said, it's good to know that if this TV-career lark all went pear-shaped, I could go back to teaching. Though, to be honest, I don't think I really want to be a teacher at 57.

Eventually I was desperate to do something different and salvation came in the form of an impromptu lesson from the school nurse – she was studying for a Legal Practice Course (LPC) for intending solicitors. When I started reading some of the textbooks, I thought to myself, 'I can do this.' I had been saving for a while, so with £20,000 in savings, I spent two years at the University of Glamorgan studying law.

MY QUIZZING CAREER BEGINS

Okay, okay, enough about my doomed career paths. You don't really want to know about all this. I suspect you'd rather find out about how I became this superstar quizzer so perhaps you can one day follow in my quizzing footsteps.

The defining moment that my quiz career took off came in late 1995. I was playing in a pub quiz at the Heath Hotel in Cardiff and, as you'd expect, doing pretty well. Eric, the landlord at the time, noticed my ability and set me up with a couple of guys he'd recently met with similar quizzing skills in a pub team for the Cardiff league.

Now I thought I was pretty good but my two new team-mates, Gary Dermott and Richie Parnell, were something else, as they were quite possibly the smartest people I had ever met. So together we started quizzing on the southwest scene, and for me it was like a post-graduate course in how to become a professional quizzer. The number of things I learned from those two guys was immense. I learned that when you get an answer wrong, you'll never get it wrong again. Hanging around good players, I soon realized, meant I got better and it wasn't long before we became a force to be reckoned with on the south Wales quiz leagues. Whenever we'd rock up to a competition and slay a bunch of teams, people would go: 'Yeah, you're decent, but this or that team are brilliant.' So we'd go and play them and beat them, which resulted in our team – the Anthill Mob, as we branded ourselves – winning lots of Welsh titles as well as a slew of UK ones and gaining quite a reputation. This encouraged us to take quizzing seriously. We were a competitive bunch for sure, we wanted to win, even if the big prize was just £500 or a thousand, which would pay for a few rounds of drinks or a small holiday. Sometimes it was just the three of us, sometimes we'd be part of a bigger team, but we were always the core of it and the ones who answered the most questions. As the Anthill Mob made its mark on the quizzing scene, the few mates I had who didn't share my love for games told me they reckoned I was becoming too obsessed. I simply replied: 'Maybe, but I enjoy it.'

GOING ON TV

Having conquered the quizzing circuit, I started to think about trying my luck on the major TV quiz shows that I had watched religiously for years. However, my sole motive was to win big money. What's the point otherwise? I kept being told I could go on *Mastermind*, but I didn't want to do that. There's no money in it, so why bother? There were plenty of other shows that offered contestants the chance to win stupid amounts of money.

But after much egging on from my mates, I did try out for *Mastermind* in 2000. Only it was the short-lived reboot of the classic show that aired on the Discovery Channel, hosted not by Magnus Magnusson or John Humphrys, but by sarky telly host Clive Anderson. If I'm honest, I went into the show half-hearted. Not only did I have no real financial incentive, but I was also busy teaching, so I didn't have the time to prepare. I chose the Olympic Games as my specialist subject and did okay on it, but I had too much to make up for on the general knowledge round. I'm going to be honest with you, I have a love/hate relationship with *Mastermind*. Yes, it is an incredibly prestigious institution. At the same time, it's almost unique in quiz shows as you're not facing your opponents, because each of you has got your own set of questions, and there's nothing you can do about the opponent. You just hope that on your set of questions you get a better score than they do.

In the summer of 2000, I took part in a touring version of *Who Wants to Be a Millionaire?* in Torquay. The various winners from around the country were invited back to the final where one person out of the three hundred would get to play for real money. Eamonn Holmes was the jovial host and guess who the lucky person plucked from the 300 was – yep, you guessed it, ME! I started off pretty well, and then stalled at £16,000 when I was asked a question I wasn't sure about. Gingelly is another name for what type of oil? In my desperate state, I took the 50-50, but that didn't help. I phoned a friend, but Richie Parnell didn't know. So it came down literally to a choice of olive oil or sesame oil. After a bit of thought, I decided the word sounded Italian and olive oil is olive oil. If the prize money hadn't been so high – it amounted to a teacher's annual salary after tax – I would have taken a blind guess and opted for sesame oil. But I didn't want to take a chance at losing it so took the money instead. Afterwards I looked up the answer – it was indeed sesame oil.

I actually appeared on *Who Wants to Be a Millionaire?* a few years later. It's funny to think that now I am in the same dressing room filming *The Chase* as I was when I was a contestant on that show. I had a great time, even though I only came away with £32,000. The question that got me? I just didn't know the answer. I could have guessed blindly, but played it safe instead as £32,000 isn't to be sniffed at! It was two years' salary after tax, thanks very much. It was more money than I'd ever seen before. What made the experience all the more enjoyable was sparring with Chris Tarrant, who at that point was in his pomp – he was possibly the best game show host in the world!

Another classic quiz show I appeared on was *Countdown*, and I had a great experience. To be honest, I wasn't great with the words, but I got both maths problems right. As a maths teacher, it could have been embarrassing had I got them wrong. Unfortunately, my opponent beat me in the final Countdown Conundrum. The word was ACQUIRING, which I was never going to get as I thought the word had two Cs! But it was a bit of fun, a day out from the school and I got to meet the wonderful Carol Vorderman. Funnily enough, after that appearance we kept bumping into each other and soon became friends. She's one of the few people who are smarter than me. My IQ is 151, hers is 154. When we get together it's like a comedy sketch as we're forever completing each other's sentences.

In 2007, I took part in the BBC's big-budget show *The People's Quiz*. Hosted by Kate Garraway, Myleene Klass and the late William G Stewart, it had been pitched as 'The Q Factor' – like *The X Factor* of quizzes – and offered contestants the chance of taking home a whopping £200,000.

Just like *The X Factor*, viewers watched quizzers 'audition' to land a place in the final 48. It was all very dramatic, as you can imagine. After my screen test, I had to wait in isolation to discover my fate. It was, I admit, quite tense. We weren't allowed access to a phone or to speak to the other hopefuls, so as time ticked by all the uncertainties started to kick in. Of course, that's exactly what the producers wanted. They wanted us whipped up into a heightened emotional state so that we'd collapse with joy or despair when they told us if we were through or not.

Apparently hundreds of hopefuls had tried out for the show, but only 48 people from around the country would be selected, before being dramatically cut down to 24 and then losing people one by one until a winner was found.

While this was happening around me, I got the feeling the show's concept wasn't entirely fair. The producers wanted to have an equal number of men and women in each of the four age categories. There were eight men and eight women in the 16–23-year-old category, the same again in the 24–39 group and the same again in the 40-plus category. This meant that the show was favouring the younger crowd, who were the most vulnerable of the lot. You see, when we got to the final 24, I could tell that most of the people in the younger category weren't really good enough to be top 24 players, while some of the older ones who'd been discarded had been.

And what happened? Well, the older, more experienced quizzers in the mix totally demolished the weaker players, mainly because we were allowed to choose who we took on. For example, there was a lovely 18-year-old girl who I picked to go head to head with and then absolutely destroyed. It wasn't her fault, at my age I just had an unfair advantage, but it was cruel. The producers had told her she was among the top 24 quizzers in the country and that I was a big bully and that she stood every chance of beating me. My mate Gary was in the audience, heard that and thought: 'Are you kidding?' He knew how much I had achieved and that I lived and breathed quizzes, and this girl had entered the show simply because it looked like fun. He actually turned to her mother and warned her: 'Brace yourself.'

It might have looked like an unfair advantage giving me the chance to destroy my rivals, but that was the way the game was set up. If you wanted to scoop the prize money, you simply couldn't afford to let anyone stay in the game, you had to put them out as quickly as you could. And so I did. She never got a chance to hit the buzzer. I don't think the producers understood the psychology of what the stronger players were doing. I think they thought we would take on people who challenged us – but with £200,000 at stake, my plan was to pick off the easiest opponents one by one. The producers just didn't get that this strategy was within the rules, and after seven weeks of contestants picking the weakest opponent, it became clear that they had made a mistake.

Afterwards I explained my game plan to the producers. 'Imagine it's the FA Cup draw,' I said. 'You're Manchester United and the FA tells you that you can pick your opponents in the next round. Are you going to pick Arsenal or Accrington Stanley?' The wave of realization that swept across their faces made it quite evident they knew where they had gone wrong.

Sadly I didn't scoop the £200,000 – I came second to a lady called Stephanie Bruce. In hindsight, I was pretty devastated because the winner went home with the £200,000 while the runner-up – me! – went home empty-handed. That said, my appearance on *The People's Quiz* helped to build a reputation that ultimately enabled me to get the job as a Chaser.

THE CHASE

Ah yes, *The Chase*. The show that turned me into a household name and the show I almost missed out on.

Nobody remembers how my name was put under the producers' noses. In the early stages of making the show, the producers wanted to have the cream of the crop of quizzers as Chasers so approached various *Mastermind* winners, which is how they stumbled across Shaun. But as anyone who watches *Mastermind* will know, the contestants get picked solely for their specialist subjects so tend to be introverts who don't make great telly, with the exception of my old mate Shaun, of course, who is the nicest guy you'll ever meet and is a wonderful, kind-hearted man.

Eventually, the producers decided they weren't finding what they were looking for in *Mastermind* winners and started to look further afield into who was doing well on the national quiz circuit. They wanted someone who was a decent player who was a bit controversial and perhaps a little bit scary and intimidating. Oddly enough, my name was mentioned.

I was invited to meet the producers for a chat but I cancelled on them because I was busy travelling with some mates and was experiencing some bad motorway problems that would mean I would be hours late. To be honest, I didn't really understand what I was being invited to and actually wondered if it was worth my while travelling up from Wales to audition for some quiz show only to be told no. So I passed.

Then a few months later, *The Chase* was announced and I kicked myself because it was then I realized the interview I had ditched had been for a proper professional gig and not just the chance to appear on a show as a contestant. So, without further ado, I got on the phone and managed to get an audition. Everyone had gone in wearing suits or jackets or their best sweaters but I turned up wearing an old Soviet-style army coat that was billowing behind me like Superman's cape. I had to duck under the doorframe and came striding in like a professional wrestler. The minute Sue Allison the producer saw me, she said: 'You've got the job!'

Sue is a lovely woman and has since revealed in a podcast that she'd originally seen me audition for *Poker Face*, a show I had applied for but didn't get on. She said that I hadn't made it that time because I was far too arrogant. She was convinced I would win but thought the public would hate it if I won £1 million. A couple of years later when she was casting *The Chase* she thought of me and said: 'That Mark Labbett guy would be effing perfect!'

You see, to be a Chaser you have to be larger than life and put on a show. A bit like WWE stars such as Steve Austin. I remember reading that his ex-wife said about him that 'the best wrestlers are themselves, but with the volume turned up,' and that's exactly what I am on *The Chase*. I am still me, just with the volume up. In fact, Oliver Reed's character in *Gladiator* sums it up best: 'I wasn't the best gladiator because I killed the quickest. I was the best because the crowd love me.' And I think I'm the same. I'm the best Chaser because the crowd love me and my ferocious competitiveness.

I think my many years of teaching experience also really helped me create my on-screen persona because I confidently spoke to the contestants like they were naughty Year 11 pupils on a wet Wednesday afternoon. I'd put them down without using bad language. To be honest, I fitted into the role straight away. I understood from the off what it was I had to do. It took some of my colleagues a bit longer to get into the swing of things. At the start, we were told not to be pantomime villains but that changed over time and we gradually mutated, because that was what the public seemed to like. When all is said and done, it's a fun show with a serious quiz at the end which audiences just love.

MEETING THE CHASERS

Bradley Walsh is a brilliant host. He was a well-known name, so he gave the show a bit of gravitas right from the start. I think one of the defining moments of *The Chase* was when I told him my name's Mark Labbett and he said: 'Where's that from?' And I said it was a French name that meant The Beast. So from that moment on he started calling me Beastie Boy. This was nothing new, as I had been called The Beast for 20-odd years on the quizzing circuit. But it was because of this nickname that every other Chaser in the world now has a nickname too.

The nicknames took a while to bed in – if you look back at season one, Shaun isn't referred to as The Dark Destroyer yet. Most people probably won't remember that the first series featured just Shaun and me, and that there were only ten episodes. For series two the producers decided to add a female Chaser to the mix and drew up a list of four. I'd met Anne Hegerty at the World Quizzing Championships just after I had filmed the first series. I'd seen her scores on the national circuit and thought: 'Wow, who's this?' Because you don't normally see people go straight into the top ten like she had. We were chatting one day and I told her she ought to apply for this show called *The Chase*. She had an interesting personality and she was a really good quizzer. Luckily the producers loved her.

Paul Sinha, a stand-up comedian, joined in series four, while Jenny Ryan, also a comic and the country's second-best female quizzer after Anne, came later. As the series went from strength to strength, the producers wanted to create a Cinderella moment by giving a worthy contestant the chance to become a Chaser – and that's how Darragh Ennis joined in 2017.

It was important to introduce new Chasers because filming episodes really took it out of us. In the early days we each did a block of three shows in a day, but it soon became obvious it was hard for us to keep up that level of concentration. The producers realized that they needed three or four of us to record enough shows a day to meet the schedule, and so we now film three episodes on three separate days. Using your brain can be harder work than people think. The concentration we need for the two-minute final Chase leaves us totally fatigued afterwards.

Maintaining concentration on the show can be difficult. Sometimes you see your colleagues, especially those who are just starting out, looking at the clock, which leads to them making a mistake, because they've just let their attention wander for a little bit. We see it with the contestants all the time: they can find it quite tough to stay focused for two minutes and you can see them start to drift off and lose their concentration.

I am very competitive, and when I sit in the hot seat on the show I want to put on my best performance. To do that I need full concentration, so that I can focus on taking on my competitors. This means I have to zone out of what is happening in the studio – I ignore the audience, the lights and the crew, clear my mind and get ready to Chase! And then when Bradley starts to fire questions at me I'm really locked in and won't notice anything other than the sound of his voice. Of course there are times when I may not be on my A-game and I'm distracted. A few years ago I lost a game when one of the camera people in the studio slipped off his podium and made a noise. It immediately broke my concentration and I did a full-on Colin Montgomerie-style side-eye stare at them and I lost. They apologized to me but I admitted that I had been struggling that day because I was half a second late on every answer. My brain hadn't been as focused as it should have been. I said to the guy: 'If I had been focused, I would never have heard the noise.'

Although we don't go head to head on the show, us Chasers are quite competitive. We all want to be the one with the most wins. But in spite of our sparring, we have always stayed on friendly terms. We are quite professional like that. While there are times on *Beat the Chasers* when I might say something that's quite sharp, after the show we're all mates again.

Although I like to win, I know that there may be times when the contestants will beat me. The first time you get stuffed as a Chaser, you find out a bit about who you are. It's like when things go wrong for a sportsperson: there's nowhere to hide, you've just got to shake your opponent by the hand, say 'Well played' and then have your tantrum backstage.

A lot of people are desperate to get on *The Chase* to take us on. They say to me: 'Oh, I'd love to go on the show. I went to the audition, but somebody worse than me got on.' But you see, it's not just about being a good quizzer. The key word there is 'audition' – you have to market yourself. You need to stand out and shine, so share a funny story about yourself – even if it's not true. I remember this one guy came on the show whose team won £40,000. He had been a *Mastermind* semi-finalist, so had form. Before the show, he had told the researchers that he planned to donate his winnings to his cricket club. After the win, the researcher said to him: 'Your cricket club must be so happy,' and he laughed and said without a shred of sheepishness: 'Nah, I've just left my wife and I need the ten grand to shack up with my girlfriend.' The producer was mortified. And I was like: 'Would you have given them a spot if they had told the truth?'

CHASE-WORTHY CHASERS

Over the years I have seen many good contestants appear on the show, but I have yet to see someone who is a match for us. Actually, I tell a lie. When I appeared on the first US version of *The Chase* back in 2014, there was a guy called James Holzhauer who was fast, knowledgeable and had something about him. At the time I remember tweeting that I reckoned he was good enough to be a Chaser. Producers interviewed him but felt his personality wasn't quite ready yet. But five years later, James is now a Chaser on the ABC version of the show.

What changed was that in 2019, he broke just about every record going on a show called *Jeopardy!* – which is an institution in the US –

and he was snapped up. In fact, producers of *The Chase USA* now look to *Jeopardy!* for the top-level Chasers. But back here in Britain, we're yet to see someone who is at our level. We do get good players on, though we haven't had a *Mastermind* champion yet, just a few finalists. But we've had people who have won *University Challenge*, *Only Connect* and *Brain of Britain*, all of whom have put up a good fight.

Paul is absolutely brilliant right now, he's consistently in the top 50 in the world and he's won the British Quiz Championship. He's a very, very good player. And, as he points out, in his opinion, if we're up against a half-decent pub quiz team, they're going to beat us because four good players are going to be too strong for us. Generally, the rule on *The Chase* is that on each team, there are two good players and two, how should I say, *characters* – but then we're an 'every person' show, that's what it's designed to be.

I can't remember experiencing too many cock-ups over the years, but there have been times when I won a show and then discovered that one of the answers I gave was wrong. Filming is all done in real time and independent adjudicators watch closely to ensure all the answers we give are correct. The adjudicators are our referees, they're all lawyers and it's their job to make sure the shows are as fair as possible for the contestants. It's something that more television quiz shows should do, because in the bad old days, the producers were effectively judge, jury and executioner.

There have been times when I felt like I didn't get something right and asked them to go back and check the answer. I remember during one final Chase I said 'Nightmare *in* Elm Street' instead of 'Nightmare *on* Elm Street' but it had slipped by unnoticed. Afterwards, I asked if we could look back at the footage, where we all saw the error. We had to refilm the final Chase from the point of that mistake and carry on with a new set of questions. More fool me, as this time I lost! But it was the only fair way of doing it. I'm paid by the production company for the series, so in theory it doesn't matter if I win or lose, the fee is the same – though of course it does matter to me.

THE PRICE OF FAME

After a few years, *The Chase* became one of the most popular shows in the UK, sometimes even getting higher ratings than the primetime soaps. The public really engaged with the show and took it to their hearts, and the other Chasers and I became household names.

It was a slow, steady climb to the top rather than an overnight success, and the show only won its first National Television Award in 2016. And yet for a while, a lot of people in the industry didn't pay us much attention, even though we had captured the nation's hearts. I used to joke that we were the best show that people had never heard of. I remember one time when we were filming at the old ITV studios on London's South Bank, Anne got stopped by security, who didn't believe she worked on the show. It was only when she pointed out her picture on the wall that they realized their error. In fact, up until recently I still had senior people at ITV asking me: 'Do you ever get recognized in a supermarket?' And I was like: 'Are you kidding me?'

The great public response reflects the fact that we are an 'every person' show. *The Chase* is the first show in a long while that actually gets the whole family watching. So when I'm out and about, I get mums and grans coming up to me in the supermarket. But I also have a massive student fanbase, probably because of the time the show airs. As I result, I get booked for nightclub gigs, which can be pretty wild. I'll rock up to the venue at around 2am and take maybe 200 pictures with lads and lasses who might have had a bit to drink. I remember at one public appearance I did in Brighton, a tipsy young lady whispered in my ear: 'You're just my type.' And my response was: 'What, fat, middle-aged and married?'

Another benefit of being 'a face off the telly' is that it can be an icebreaker. A few years back, some mates and I were out on the town in Sheffield and two attractive blondes sidled over to us and asked for a photo with me. My mate Brett, who'd been at the bar to get the drinks, saw them and dashed back at warp speed. The next thing I know, he and this young lady, who was called Nicola, were completely consumed with each other as if the rest of the world didn't matter. Before long, the pair of them ended up in what could only be described as a make-out session. The reason I mention this story is because nine years later Brett and Nicola are still together and have two beautiful kids.

On the whole, I really enjoy meeting interesting people at parties, especially when they already know my name, which I still find very weird. I also get to meet people I've admired for years. I once met Sean Bean at an event and was absolutely starstruck. And when I was working on the American version of *The Chase*, not only was the show's host, Brooke Burns, an ex-*Baywatch* girl, but I also got to meet David Hasselhoff. I couldn't believe it. I was like: 'Hang on a minute, I'm working with a *Baywatch* girl and I've just met the Hoff!' This was the stuff dreams are made of. Then an hour later, we met John Ratzenberger, who played Cliff in *Cheers*, and Gary Busey, and it was all so surreal. I remember thinking to myself that just a few years earlier, at that very time of day, I'd have been in a classroom that I thought I was going to spend the rest of my working life in.

Fame is a funny thing, because I'm still the person I was before I went on TV. I just earn a lot more money and people treat me differently. I try not to get carried away but sometimes the trappings of fame do tickle me. During a trip to New York, I was offered a VIP tour of the Empire State Building. While we were waiting to go up in the lift to take in the panoramic views of the Big Apple, a load of British tourists passed by and all started taking my photo. The chief usher who was showing us around was astounded and asked: 'Who the hell are you?' When he found out I was on British TV, we got the real VIP tour! Another champagne moment was when my mate Carol Vorderman sent me a text message saying: 'I'm in Times Square and there's a 40 foot poster of you here.' I was gobsmacked.

This is, of course, all weird for someone who never expected to be on TV. In fact, no one I know ever expected me to end up doing what I do. So imagine how bizarre it was for me not only to attend the BAFTA TV Awards in 2022 but also to have our show announced as a winner. I was thrilled, of course. It was brilliant that we had been considered the best in the Daytime category but I'm not the type to get too emotional about these things, so I kept a stiff upper lip. The producers and Paul Sinha, on the other hand, were all in tears, while I laughed: 'Ugh, it's just a lump of lead.' Besides, it's not as if the Chasers got to keep any of the five gongs – we only got to hold them for the press pics.

Of course, as much joy as fame can bring, it can also prove to be rather irritating. I love people but if a drunk person starts to bother me, it's time for me to go because they can get aggy under the influence. Fortunately, I've got good friends who keep an eye out for troublesome folks and suggest we move on when someone starts to kick off. Who knows what will happen? You might as well just buy the bloody drink and move on.

Another downside of being 'famous' is that the press are always after a story, which is why I tend to stay sober at public events. At the BAFTAs, for example, I got buttonholed by some tabloid journalists and, while they were lovely, they'd all had a bit to drink. ITV had sent PRs along to look after us on the red carpet, to make sure we didn't say anything we shouldn't, but by that stage of the evening they were basically getting squiffy themselves. Luckily, I'm a canny lad, and I could see all the traps coming – you know, questions like: 'What do you think about your colleagues?' So I was very careful and didn't say anything that would get me into trouble. I must admit the one naughty thing I did was slightly exaggerate how much money I made on the American show, knowing it would get in the paper, because you set your level for the next gig. My agent wasn't best pleased.

THE CHASE USA

I can quite safely say that *The Chase* has changed my life. No longer a frustrated teacher, I've had doors open to me that I would never have expected. One of those doors led me to the US where I was asked to join the American version of *The Chase*. I did it in two batches. The first series I did was in 2014, on the Game Show Network. I'm not going to lie, I was offered a lot of money to do it so it was a no-brainer. To start with I had a lot of fun but, as is so often the way, the network had a change in management, and whenever that happens the new management want to make their mark and bring in new shows, so they stopped making *The Chase*.

In 2020, one of the bigger networks, ABC, picked up and rebooted *The Chase*. Again I was invited to join an all-American cast of Chasers and I had the best time, and not just because the fee they offered me was obscene. In fact, it was so much money that if I had a problem with the production I actually kept my mouth shut. That said, looking back there were one or two things that I wish I had spoken up about.

As time went on, the producers tried to take the show in a younger direction, employing younger question writers and including questions about 'Internet memes', social media and stuff like that, which I was struggling with then. To begin with I was worried and thought I was out of my depth. I started to think: 'If you're going to be asking questions with a young viewer in mind, why bother employing me?' Sure, I'm an all-rounder, but there are certain things a 56-year-old man is less likely to be knowledgeable about. But then when I discovered my three American colleagues were struggling as well, I felt reassured.

My biggest issue was that a lot of the questions were based around US culture – like adverts that we don't get in the UK. I just didn't have knowledge. That said, whenever there were any questions about the rest of the world or Europe, I was banging the answers off with ease, and my fellow Chasers would be like: 'How do you know that?' But in truth, the questions were just plain hard. There were so many that both the Chasers and the contestants simply didn't know the answer to.

While I didn't return to the US version of the *The Chase*, I still appear on the Australian version. Years ago, an Aussie network started to show the UK version at 3pm. It was a smash hit, so they decided to make their own version and asked Anne and me to fly across the world to become Chasers. I actually missed the first series back in 2015, because the producers of the first incarnation of the US series persuaded me not to do it – they kept telling me they wanted to hire me for the US series that same summer. When I heard no word about that series, I cut my losses and joined the second series of the Australian series alongside Anne.

Since then, I've done around seven or eight series, so have notched up quite a lot of air miles. Anne has done about nine or ten, because up until recently they had no Australian women on the show. Shaun came over for one series as a guest Chaser, but Anne and I are part of the core line-up.

BEAT THE CHASERS

On the teatime version of *The Chase*, each Chaser takes on the public on our own – we're the Alpha quizzer. While we might be competitive about how many times we stop the public from winning the jackpot, we're never in direct competition with one another. So when the idea of *Beat the Chasers* came up it was a whole new proposition. Suddenly we were on a team of five or six Chasers taking on members of the public. Playing against the clock, we had to buzz in to ensure we got as many right answers as possible to stop our opponent winning the money. This took some getting used to, and I would get irritated if one of the others buzzed in ahead of me and got the answer wrong. So during the game I would be visibly frustrated if someone made a silly mistake, but then backstage I'd put my arm around them and talk about how we can be better.

If I'm honest, I think I prefer the regular Chase myself, because you know where you are with it. *Beat the Chasers* takes the power away from us – the producers pick the Chasers, the times offered, the amounts of money. I know it's a handicap game but suddenly that's a pretty big handicap we've got to try and chase down.

CHASERS ROAD TRIP

Another show that came off the back of *The Chase* was *The Chasers Road Trip*, which in my mind was the opposite of *An Idiot Abroad*. The show featured Anne, Shaun and myself, and we hadn't been told beforehand what we were getting into so everything came as a surprise. We didn't have an itinerary, it was just like: 'Okay, what are we doing today?' kind of thing. We had a great time filming the series and along the way we got to learn certain things about ourselves. Or at least confirmed things I already knew!

In one episode, the three of us took an IQ test. Shaun wasn't too concerned about gaining a high score because he knew that his way of finding things out was through research and response, but of course I was curious and very keen to have a high score. As expected, Shaun was told his full-scale IQ was 96, on a par with 70 per cent of the population. Anne fared better with a score of 137, which put her in the top 1 per cent. I had 151, which put me in super-smug mode. In three of the ten categories used to judge our IQ, the psychologists said: 'He's not just in the top 1 per cent. He is the top of the top 1 per cent.'

While Anne and I had high IQ scores, we were told we had a very low emotional IQ. The psychologist told us competitiveness wasn't great for our psyche, at which point I thought to myself: 'Do you know what we do?' I scored 6 per cent and, if I'm honest, I was so proud of that, because I answered what I believed. Conversely, I got 97 per cent for my self-esteem, which I was told was dangerously high. Of course, when you've been told you've scored 97 per cent for self-esteem, the only thing you're thinking is, where did I lose the 3 per cent? But this does go to show that I have a totally different mindset to some people and I think viewers can see that. They can see that I'm serious about what I do. I play to win.

Later on in the trip, we all had an MRI scan that merely proved that our brains showed no signs of anything unusual, so we have no real idea why we are the way we are. However, we did find out one very interesting quirk which may or may not be significant. We were only tested for one night but all three of us experienced significantly more of the deepest sleep state (D3) – which is the one associated with memory, creation and retention – than would be expected of people our age. This was curious and it raises the question, do our brains need more D3 sleep to process our memories, or does a natural excess of D3 sleep lead us to have superior memories? I don't have the answer, so I'll leave that to the experts to work out. But just imagine how great it would be if somebody came up with a pill or a method to give you an extra couple of hours of deep sleep a night, and you suddenly found you could remember everything.

As I mentioned earlier, there has been discussion about whether or not I may be on the autism spectrum. I don't know. The jury is out. I clearly have some of the traits associated with being on the spectrum, in particular a liking for facts, mental arithmetic and my own company. However, I am pretty good at thinking on my feet whereas a lot of neurodiverse people are easily thrown by surprises. I was offered a chance to be diagnosed properly recently, but it would have cost something like two grand. I didn't need to know that badly, because, if I am on the autistic spectrum, I am pretty high-functioning.

Anne has spoken about having Asperger's, which is a type of autism, and I'm very protective of her. We get on really well and she's godmother to my son. People don't realize that autism is not just a label. For example, there's definitely a limit to how much time Anne can spend in the company of other people before she shuts down. When we'd arrive back at the hotel after a day of filming on the road, I would urge the producers to let her go straight to her room to have some time to be on her own. She's not being anti-social, she just needs to have a couple of hours to herself, and then she can deal with being around people again. One of the most fascinating conversations I've ever witnessed was between Anne, Robbie Williams and his wife Ayda. They were discussing Robbie's coping strategies when dealing with the public. Before they start, they said, they set a time of how long they are going to do it for. And that's just like Anne. When we attend award ceremonies and she's said she's had enough of schmoozing, I get her out of there fast!

HAVING A FAMILY

Earlier I explained that during my younger years, I didn't really have much of a romantic life. But in 2013, I met someone and we got married and had a son, Lawrence. To be honest, married life was hard to start with as I'd been a single man for a long while. Sharing your life with someone can be tough after having been a bachelor for so long, because it's so easy to become selfish about your time and doing what you want to do all the time. Things weren't always easy, just like in any marriage, and sadly we eventually went our separate ways, though we still have a strong relationship for the sake of our son.

I have to admit though that when you open your life up to a relationship or to parenthood, it does become harder to be a quizzer. When you're in a relationship, your time isn't quite as free as when you're on your own so you've got to manage your time carefully. It's hard to concentrate when just as you settle down you hear 'Daddy!' Or you find that you want to watch something for research purposes and realize you can't really have it on in the background because it's rated 12 or 15, and there might be particularly gratuitous violence or sex or bad language. That's when I have to be a daddy. So for the most part I spend the evenings with Lawrence and then after he has gone to bed, I will get on with what I need to do. The problem is these days, when he goes to bed, I'm generally asleep about an hour later.

Lawrence is five now and he's enjoying school. Whether he will follow in my footsteps, I'm not sure. I don't think he's going to be quite like me. He's more of an architect or engineer type. Funnily enough, though, I chatted to his teacher a while back and we both said independently that we think he's got an exceptional memory, which means that whatever he's interested in, he'll be really good at. So who knows, he may grow up to be a genius quizzer like his dad. And then what? As I always say to the producers, me and the current Chasers still have about 20 years in us but one day I look forward to retiring and will be happy when my son is ready to take over my job. They have a good laugh, but I'm only half joking when I say that.

GENERAL KNOWLEDGE: EASY

GENERAL KNOWLEDGE 1

1. The 2018 UK Christmas number one by LadBaby mentioned which food?

2. What was the name of the show conceived by Michael Flatley as a follow-up to *Riverdance* – it also gave Flatley his nickname?

3. Who first came into the UK public eye when he played Scott Robinson on *Neighbours*?

4. What relation to you is your son's grandfather's brother?

5. Which group's only UK number one was 'The Final Countdown'?

6. *Rear Guard* was the failed US adaptation of which British comedy?

7. The Great Barrier Reef is made primarily from which substance?

8. The holy book the Qu'ran is written in which language?

9. Comice and Bartlett are varieties of which fruit?

10. Boise is the capital of which US state?

11. Which cocktail in its most basic form contains vodka, Galliano and orange juice?

12. What would be your star sign if you were born on April Fools' Day?

13. Which song from the musical *Carousel* is used as the unofficial anthem of Liverpool FC?

14. What name is given to a triangle with three internal angles that are all the same?

15. Temple Meads railway station can be found in which English city?

16. Which pass links Afghanistan and Pakistan through the Spīn Ghar mountains?

17. What precise colour was the boat in which the Owl and the Pussycat went to sea?

18. Famous for their Crispy Pancakes, which company was embroiled in the 2013 horse-meat scandal?

19. What is the main ingredient of hummus?

20. Which establishment benefits from the profits made by the novel *Peter Pan*?

21. What naval measurement is equal to a tenth of a nautical mile?

22. Bibendum is the correct name of which famous advertising mascot?

23. On which day are American Presidential elections always held?

24. Which breed of dog was named after a German tax collector?

25. In his will, William Shakespeare famously left his wife his second-best what?

26. A rikishi is a competitor in which sport?

27. In January 2004, which pop star was married to Jason Alexander for 55 hours?

28. In which year did Alcatraz prison officially close?

29. In the nursery rhyme and singing game 'Oranges and Lemons', how much do you owe to the bells of St Martin's?

30. Common in hymns, which word comes from the Aramaic meaning 'save, rescue or saviour'?

GENERAL KNOWLEDGE 2

1. According to the prison-based Netflix TV show, what colour is the new black?

2. A leapling is a person born on which date?

3. What is the world's most common bird, and also the most commonly eaten bird?

4. Which is the second largest of the Channel Islands?

5. What drink is made by mixing lager and cider in equal measures?

6. The Russian city of St Petersburg was known by what name between 1924 and 1991?

7. Which saint guards the pearly gates and allows entrance to heaven?

8. What name is given to a musical group consisting of four players?

9. Along with Portugal, which country makes up the Iberian Peninsula?

10. Which day of the week appears in the title of singles by Blondie, Oasis, Small Faces and Morrissey?

11. What electric quantity is measured in amperes?

12. Which flower is the first name of Mrs Bucket in the sitcom *Keeping Up Appearances?*

13. The Uffington White Horse is a chalk figure found in which English county?

14. What name is given to writing that appears raised on a piece of paper or card? The same name is also used to describe wallpaper that is raised from the surface of the wall.

15. Originally called Les Schtroumpfs, what series of blue characters was created by the comics artist Peyo in 1958?

16. Which is the first dance mentioned in the NATO phonetic alphabet?

17. How many kilobytes are there in a gigabyte?

18. Which item of confectionery was 'made to make your mouth water'?

19. Which Shakespearean character has a wife called Desdemona?

20. If two standard six-sided dice are rolled, what is the probability that the total shown is seven?

21. Clacket Lane and South Mimms are service stations situated on which British motorway?

22. In which Asian country is Tagalog spoken?

23. What seafood would you receive if you ordered *pulpo* in a Spanish bar or restaurant?

24. The musical film *The Greatest Showman*, starring Hugh Jackman, is based on the life of which person?

25. Whose statue near Trinity College Dublin is referred to by locals as 'The Tart with the Cart'?

26. What is the correct name of the void created when water drains down a plughole?

27. What is the first name of Jane Austen's character Mr Darcy?

28. Which nautical punishment involved a person being dragged beneath a ship while at sea?

29. As the lead singer of Motörhead, how was Ian Kilmister better known?

30. Prior to adding two red stripes in 2017, which African country was one of only two nations (alongside Jamaica) not to have any red, white or blue on its flag?

GENERAL KNOWLEDGE 3

1. 'If you have a problem, if no one else can help, and if you can find them', then maybe you could hire whom, on TV in the 1980s?

2. Which US state lends its name to a baked pudding, made with ice cream, sponge and meringue?

3. In the Harry Potter books, what is the first name of Draco Malfoy's father?

4. What is the name of the character played by Marcia Cross in the television programme *Desperate Housewives*?

5. In which stage and film musical does Danny Zuko appear?

6. Which military facility in Cuba was known by the nickname 'Gitmo'?

7. Which footballer was famously mentioned in adverts for milk (alongside Accrington Stanley)?

8. Gin is made from the berries of which plant?

9. Which comedian told of the Diddy Men and their work in the Jam Butty mines?

10. Sugarloaf Mountain overlooks which city?

11. In Scrabble, how many points are scored for the word 'yak', with no double or triple scores involved?

12. The *Titanic* was built at the Harland & Wolff shipyard in which city?

13. From which flower is the spice saffron obtained?

14. Which disease of the eye can be categorized as 'open-angle' or 'closed-angle'?

15. Which band topped the charts with 'Sex on Fire'?

16. What name is given to a mythical creature with the body of a lion and the head and wings of an eagle?

17. Somnambulation is the medical name for which commonly late-night condition?

18. Wyoming is the final US state alphabetically – which is the next-to-last?

19. The sum of the coins in circulation in Britain is £3.88 (£2 + £1 + 50p + 20p + 10p + 5p + 2p + 1p). What is the equivalent sum in the US?

20. Which branch of medicine deals with the study of the central nervous system?

21. Which rule of football was number nine in the 1856 list of 'Cambridge Rules'?

22. What chain of restaurants was founded in Guiseley, Yorkshire, in the 1920s?

23. Whose best-selling memoir, published in 2007, was entitled *My Booky Wook?*

24. Timmy is the dog in the *Famous Five* novels. What is the name of the dog in the *Secret Seven* books?

25. The highest award given by the country of Denmark is the order of which animal?

26. Who, in the Book of Genesis, becomes the first drunken man after planting a vineyard?

27. In which town in the northwest of England was DJ and presenter Chris Evans born in 1966?

28. What was the surname of Margo and Jerry, neighbours of Tom and Barbara Good in the BBC sitcom *The Good Life?*

29. Which country is known as Suomi in its own language?

30. Echoing a stammer that he had used in his role in the BBC sitcom *All Gas and Gaiters*, which actor sang the jingle 'P-p-p-p-pick Up a Penguin'?

GENERAL KNOWLEDGE 4

1. The island of Santorini is part of which country?

2. In America it's called tic-tac-toe. What do we call it in the UK?

3. Which six-letter term is used to refer to the lower part of the back? It can precede 'puncture'.

4. Which bird of prey could also be fun for a child on a windy day?

5. In order to use it, what would you do to a joss stick?

6. Halitosis sufferers have what ailment?

7. Who released an app called 'Click to Pray'?

8. Born 'Bessie', what first name was Mrs Simpson better known by? She married Edward VIII after his abdication and became the Duchess of Windsor.

9. Which type of confectionery, similar to toffee, was first produced in 1848 by three rival firms in Doncaster?

10. Brothers Danny and Richard McNamara are founder members of which Yorkshire indie rock band?

11. Which famous book is preceded by *Angels and Demons* and followed by *The Lost Symbol*?

12. Who had the first new number one of the 1970s with 'Love Grows (Where My Rosemary Goes)'?

13. Which trade union leader once described Margaret Thatcher as the 'Plutonium Blonde'?

14. Majority-owned by Volkswagen, which German car company makes the Boxster, Cayman and 911?

15. Built to house the Great Exhibition of 1851 in Hyde Park, what structure was destroyed by fire in 1936?

16. Hong Kong is one of two 'special administrative regions' of China; what is the other?

17. Which eponymous comic-strip cat is owned by Jon Arbuckle?

18. Albacore, bigeye and yellowfin are examples of which type of fish?

19. Who played Pam Ewing in the original run of the TV show *Dallas*?

20. From which language do we get the word 'yoga'?

21. Which children's books character is known as 'Oui Oui' in France?

22. If you ordered *homard* in a French restaurant, what shellfish would you be served?

23. Michael Keaton, Val Kilmer, George Clooney – who comes next?

24. In Gustav Holst's 'Planets' suite, which planet is the bringer of jollity?

25. The youngest of whose six children is Chloe, born in 2003? His eldest child is Prudence, born in 1958.

26. 'Accent', as used as a flavouring by KFC, is another name for which additive?

27. On which farm did Worzel Gummidge live?

28. The 1973 US Supreme Court ruling in Roe v Wade was a landmark decision on which issue?

29. Glasgow Rangers play their home games at which stadium?

30. Whose only hit was 'Apparently Nothin'' in 1991?

GENERAL KNOWLEDGE 5

1. Who directed the films *E.T.*, *Jurassic Park*, *Schindler's List* and *Saving Private Ryan*?

2. What name is given to the diet that prohibits the consumption of not only meat but all animal by-products?

3. In which American state will you find the cities of Tampa Bay, Orlando and Miami?

4. Which planet of the solar system has a feature on it known as the Great Red Spot?

5. The countries Vatican City and San Marino are entirely surrounded by which other country?

6. Which toys that inspired a cartoon series in the 1980s and later a live-action series of films were known as robots in disguise?

7. Between 1508 and 1512, which person painted the ceiling of the Sistine Chapel?

8. Which chemical element with the atomic number 3 is the lightest metal?

9. Known for their songs 'Take on Me', 'The Sun Always Shines on TV' and the Bond theme 'The Living Daylights', the band A-ha comes from which country?

10. What alcoholic spirit features in the drink the Moscow Mule?

11. After Brazil, what is the second-largest country in South America by area?

12. What are the only mammals that are capable of true flight?

13. Which king of England was known as Longshanks and the Hammer of the Scots?

14. In which book of the Bible does the story of Noah and the flood appear?

15. What is the common name of the substance iron pyrite, which is often mistaken for another, more valuable, substance?

16. On 20 July 1944, Günther Korten, Heinz Berger, Heinz Brandt and Rudolf Schmundt were all killed by a bomb that was intended to kill which person? He survived, only suffering perforated ear drums.

17. The TV series *The Night Manager*, *Smiley's People* and *Tinker Tailor Soldier Spy* are all based on novels by which writer?

18. What animal would you find on the badge of Porsche cars?

19. Unsurprisingly, since it shares its name with the country's capital city, Windhoek Lager is the most popular lager in which African country?

20. Which country, represented by The Makemakes, in 2015 became the first and so far only host nation to receive *nul points* at the Eurovision Song Contest? In 2014, their winning entrant was Conchita Wurst.

21. Which European capital city lies on the River Manzanares?

22. What is the only novel by Charles Dickens that has two title characters?

23. What is the name of the traditional Russian tea urn that translates into English as 'self-boiler'?

24. Depression-era gangster George Barnes (1895–1954) and rapper Richard Colson Baker (born 1990) are both better known by what other name?

25. Whose five marriages were to Sharon Williams, Gale Anne Hurd, Kathryn Bigelow, Linda Hamilton and Suzy Amis?

26. 'Oh, What a Beautiful Morning' is the first song in the musical *Oklahoma!* Which character is it performed by?

27. What is the name of the syndrome, named after a Shakespearean character, where a person has a constant belief that their partner is cheating on them, despite there being no evidence to suggest it?

28. In 1901 Clement Duval became the first person to successfully escape from which French penal colony? The lead character in the film *Papillon* also escaped from this prison.

29. Published in 1967, Dodie Smith's novel *The Starlight Barking* is the sequel to which book?

30. In 1977, Bruce Wilhelm became the first person to win which annual sporting event? His competitors for the title included five-time Mr Universe Franco Colombu, future WWE Intercontinental Champion Ken Patera and Lou Ferrigno, who would go on to play the Incredible Hulk.

GENERAL KNOWLEDGE: MEDIUM

GENERAL KNOWLEDGE 6

1. In which US national park in Wyoming, Montana and Idaho would you find the geyser nicknamed 'Old Faithful'?

2. *Red Vineyard at Arles*, on display at the Pushkin Museum of Fine Arts in Moscow, is said to have been the only painting sold during the lifetime of which artist?

3. In which 1999 film did Cole Sear, played by Hayley Joel Osment, famously say: 'I see dead people'?

4. Lacryma Christi or the Tears of Christ is a wine variety made from grapes indigenous to which volcano?

5. Jean-Michel Basquiat, Banksy and Keith Haring are all names associated with which controversial art form, which takes its name from the Italian meaning 'scratched'?

6. If all the elements of the periodic table were to be listed alphabetically, which would come last?

7. Lena Headey, Charles Dance, Peter Dinklage, Jack Gleeson and Nikolaj Coster-Waldau all played members of which family in the television drama series *Game of Thrones*?

8. Which county of Northern Ireland shares its name with the second-lightest of the elementary particles known as quarks?

9. In the world of professional wrestling, what was the stage name used by Roy Wayne Farris, who dressed like Elvis Presley and carried a guitar?

10. What is the wide-brimmed hat that takes its name from the Spanish word meaning 'shade' called?

11. Cardi B and J Balvin collaborated with which Puerto Rican rapper on 'I Like It', released in 2018?

12. Which pioneer of electronic and synthesizer-inspired music wrote the scores for the films *A Clockwork Orange*, *The Shining* and *Tron*?

13. The *Sivatherium* is an extinct species of which animal? It is often described as the tallest ruminant ever to walk the earth.

14. Which song from The Beatles' *White Album* did Charles Manson say made him want to start a race war in the USA?

15. The value and quality of a diamond are determined by the four Cs. Three of the four are cut, carat and colour. What is the fourth?

16. Which actress was married to men with the surnames Hilton, Wilding, Todd, Fisher, Burton, Warner and Fortensky?

17. What is the name of the North African spice mix, whose name means 'head of the shop', that is traditionally a selection of the best spices a vendor has to offer?

18. Which musical, with music and lyrics by Stephen Schwartz, includes the songs 'I'm Not That Girl', 'Defying Gravity' and 'The Wizard and I'?

19. Pencil, mini, bubble, A-line and puffball are all types of which item of clothing?

20. In mechanics, what two-word name is given to the minimum speed needed by a free, non-propelled object to break out from the gravitational influence of a massive body?

21. By what two-word name is Sharbat Gula better known, after being featured in a photograph taken by Steve McCurry for the cover of *National Geographic* magazine in June 1985?

22. Which significant event in British history occurred between 2 and 6 September in the year that is represented by the seven Roman numerals in descending order?

23. *The Sun Also Rises* by Ernest Hemingway, *The House of Mirth* by Edith Wharton and the Pete Seeger song 'Turn, Turn, Turn' all take their titles from which book of the Bible?

24. By what name is the Kerepakupai-Merú waterfall in Venezuela better known? The world's tallest uninterrupted waterfall takes its more common name from an American pilot and explorer.

25. Which American cosmetics company, a subsidiary of L'Oréal, is perhaps best known for the Naked range including Naked Heat, Naked Cherry and Naked Honey?

26. The flag of Lebanon is comprised of red, white, red horizontal bands, with what type of tree at the centre of the white band?

27. Who wrote and performed 'Searchin' My Soul', the theme tune to the television drama *Ally McBeal*? She also appeared in the show as herself, performing as a bar singer.

28. What is the Aboriginal name of the large sandstone formation in Australia's Northern Territory, which has the alternative name Ayers Rock?

29. Which American, who was co-awarded the Nobel Memorial Prize in Economic Sciences with Britain's John Hicks in 1972, is perhaps best known for his namesake impossibility theorem?

30. The actress Grace Gummer, who married DJ and music producer Mark Ronson in 2021, is the daughter of which award-winning Hollywood actress?

GENERAL KNOWLEDGE 7

1. Which US President was assassinated in Ford's Theatre on 15 April 1865?

2. *Cat on a Hot Tin Roof* and *A Streetcar Named Desire* are plays written by which American playwright?

3. Which men's lifestyle magazine was founded by Hugh Hefner in 1953? It is known for its centrefolds and rabbit logo.

4. Which name is given to the wide, flat sheets of pasta used to make a layered Italian dish?

5. Which South African President wrote the memoir *Long Walk to Freedom*? He was the nation's first Black head of state.

6. Which sitcom, which ran from 1985 to 1992, starred Bea Arthur, Estelle Getty, Rue McClanahan and Betty White as four women living together in Miami?

7. The second voyage of which ship carried Charles Darwin around the world and gave its name to the journal that he later published? It shares its name with a breed of dog.

8. A cardiologist is a specialist in which organ?

9. Rothschild is a subspecies of which animal from the species *G. camelopardalis*?

10. Which author wrote the book *The Second Sex*?

11. Which island, in the Greater Antilles, is divided between Haiti and Dominican Republic?

12. Which drug was originally developed for chest pains? Pfizer repositioned the drug to treat erectile dysfunction.

13. Who managed Elvis Presley from 1955 to 1977? Born in the Netherlands, he was made an honorary colonel.

14. Who was the lead singer of the Spencer Davies Group? He also fronted Traffic and Blind Faith before a successful solo career with the singles 'Higher Love' and 'Roll with It'.

15. Who was the first actor to portray the Joker on the ABC series *Batman*? He starred as the Cisco Kid in Westerns made between 1939 and 1941.

16. Which 1997 Paul Thomas Anderson film stars Mark Wahlberg as Dirk Diggler, a man who becomes a porn star?

17. Which author became the first African-American woman to win the Pulitzer Prize for *The Color Purple* in 1982? She coined the term 'womanism' in her 1983 collection *In Search of Our Mothers' Gardens*.

18. Which cosmetics company has the slogan 'The Makeup of Makeup Artists'? Named after its Polish founder, the company's product line includes Facefinity and Miracle Touch.

19. Which actor has Mary Steenburgen been married to since 1995? He is best known for his roles on *Cheers* and *The Good Place*.

20. William Hartnell, Christopher Ecclestone, Sylvester McCoy and Jodie Whittaker have all played which character?

21. Which actress, who has portrayed Eve Moneypenny in Bond films since 2012, was Academy Award-nominated for her role in *Moonlight* in 2016?

22. With which neighbouring nation did Honduras have a 100-hour war after a 1969 World Cup qualifier lead to unrest?

23. Who did Mariah Carey duet with on the song 'When You Believe', released in 1998? This singer, who died in 2012, also duetted with Enrique Iglesias and George Michael.

24. Roland Ratzenberger and Ayrton Senna died on 30 April and 1 May 1994 respectively in which Grand Prix in the town of Imola?

25. What is the name of the gland found at the base of the brain? It produces the hormones that regulate functions such as growth and reproduction.

26. Jean Grey is the alter ego of which *X-Men* superhero?

27. Pico Turquino is part of the Sierra Maestra mountain range on which Caribbean island?

28. What is the condition where tissue similar to the lining of the uterus starts to grow outside of the uterus, such as in the ovaries and fallopian tubes?

29. Which songwriter has been nominated for 12 Academy Awards for Best Original Song? Her catalogue includes the songs 'How Do I Live?' and 'Because You Loved Me'.

30. Princess Leonor is the heir presumptive of which southern European nation? If she ascends the throne, she will be the nation's second queen regnant after Isabella II.

GENERAL KNOWLEDGE 8

1. James Dougherty, Joe DiMaggio and Arthur Miller were the three husbands of which actress and cultural icon?

2. Which solid form of the element carbon is found at 10 on the Mohs scale of mineral hardness?

3. *La Traviata*, *Rigoletto* and *Nabucco* are among the operas composed by which Italian?

4. What name is shared by a city on the River Tay in central Scotland and the capital of the state of Western Australia?

5. A spokesperson for which American coffee company, headquartered in Seattle, has described the company logo as 'a twin-tailed mermaid or siren, as she's known in Greek mythology'?

6. Which traditional Cuban cocktail consists of five ingredients: white rum, sugarcane juice, lime juice, soda water and mint?

7. Which Swedish scientist (1707–1778) formalized the modern system of binomial nomenclature?

8. Which character in the *Mario* series is often seen wearing a purple and yellow plumber's outfit? Known for his zigzagging moustache, he is one of Mario's main rivals.

9. Which children's television character owns machines such as Scoop, Muck, Lofty, Dizzy and Roley? He is often seen alongside his wife and business partner Wendy.

10. John Fogarty was the lead singer of which rock band known for hits such as 'Fortunate Son' and 'Bad Moon Rising'?

11. Which God-fearing neighbour of The Simpsons is often heard saying 'diddly'?

12. *The _____ Karamazov* is the final novel by the Russian author Fyodor Dostoevsky. Which family members should fill in the blank?

13. If Shiva is often seen as the destroyer and Vishnu as the preserver, which god is typically seen as the creator?

14. Viggo Mortensen stars as Tony Lip and Mahershala Ali stars as Don Shirley in which Best Picture-winning film that was directed by Peter Farrelly?

15. The Hall of Mirrors is found in a palace in which city? The peace treaty that brought World War One to an end was also signed at this location.

16. _____'s *World* is a painting by Andrew Wyeth. Which first name, which is also the first name of the singer of 'Genie in a Bottle', fills in the blank?

17. In October 2019, Dr Kristalina Georgieva took over as the managing director of which organization? For the previous eight years, the role had been filled by Christine Lagarde.

18. Until his death in 1980, Bon Scott was the lead singer and vocalist for which Australian rock band?

19. What is the capital city of Chile?

20. Marvin Hagler, Carlos Monzon and Gennady Golovkin have all been World Champion in which boxing weight class?

21. 'I'm mad as hell, and I'm not going to take this anymore' is the catchphrase of Howard Beale in which 1976 film?

22. Commonly called 'The Hell of the North' and known for its rough cobblestone terrain, the cycling 'monument' that starts in Paris finishes in which city in northern France?

23. Which word completes the full name of this sovereign state of circa 410,000 people: Nation of _____, the Abode of Peace? In recent years, this nation has come under fire for its homophobic policies.

24. Which Fritz Lang film, with a single-letter title, is widely credited with launching the career of Peter Lorre? He plays the lead role of the serial killer Hans Beckert in the film.

25. Babs Lord, Dee Dee Wilde, Ruth Pearson, Louise Clarke and Cherry Gillespie were all members of which dance troupe that appeared regularly on *Top of the Pops* between 1968 and 1976?

26. Dwayne Johnson plays the role of Maui and Auli'i Cravalho plays the title role in which 2016 Disney animated feature film?

27. The tallest statue in the world of a woman, *The Motherland Calls*, can be found in which Russian city?

28. Which hugely successful NBA franchise has had 'the Bill Russell era', 'the Larry Bird era' and, most recently, 'the Paul Pierce era'?

29. 'Through the Wire', 'Slow Jamz' and 'Jesus Walks' are all singles from which critically acclaimed debut studio album by Kanye West?

30. Which scientist won the first-ever Nobel Prize in Physics? Element 111 on the periodic table is also named after him.

GENERAL KNOWLEDGE 9

1. Clara Oswald, Amy Pond, Sarah Jane Smith, Martha Jones and Rose Tyler are all known for being a companion of whom?

2. Which song begins 'She came from Greece she had a thirst for knowledge/She studied sculpture at Saint Martin's College'?

3. In which type of receptacle does *Sesame Street* character Oscar the Grouch live?

4. What type of food is Monterey Jack?

5. Popular messaging platform Snapchat's logo consists of a silhouette of what shape?

6. Which TV programme famously broadcast the 1957 'spaghetti harvest' hoax?

7. The Palk Strait separates India from which island nation to the south?

8. Which prominent American labour union leader mysteriously disappeared after leaving a Detroit restaurant in 1975?

9. What is the official language of Mexico?

10. Which Hollywood star's name is an anagram of Germany?

11. Which liquid is made from a type of soot called lampblack, combined with water? (Two-word answer.)

12. When he failed to appear in June 1993, which politician was replaced on *Have I Got News for You* by the now iconic 'tub of lard'?

13. Which two colours are synonymous with the famous Harrods department store in Knightsbridge?

14. The capital and largest city of the Seychelles shares its name with which British queen?

15. In the Harry Potter stories, which animal is on the coat of arms of Gryffinddor house?

16. By what other name is the Bogside Massacre more commonly known? It took place on 30 January 1972.

17. Which English mill town once produced 99 per cent of the world's cotton?

18. Two African countries have a name that starts with D. The Democratic Republic of the Congo is one, what is the other?

19. Tórshavn is the capital of which island group?

20. Which Sunday staple debuted on British TV on 1 October 1961 and can still be seen (and heard) today?

21. The potential candidates to represent the UK at the 2017 Eurovision Song Contest had all been previously seen on which TV show?

22. Which title is commonly given to the speech Harold Macmillan gave to the Parliament of South Africa on 3 February 1960? The title is taken from a line in the speech.

23. Famous for his namesake dyke, Offa was the king of which Anglo-Saxon kingdom, the capital of which was Tamworth?

24. What food was used to erase lead pencil marks before rubber erasers came into use?

25. Prince Charles was the first member of the Royal Family to give what in 1985?

26. In 1999, the American Film Institute ranked the 100 greatest male screen legends of all time. Who came out top?

27. What was the John F Kennedy International Airport in New York formerly known as?

28. Which Shakespeare play does the line 'Let me have men about me that are fat' come from?

29. In a Roman house, what activity took place in the triclinium?

30. Fashion designer Oscar de la Renta was born in which Caribbean country?

GENERAL KNOWLEDGE 10

1. What nickname is given to the number 88 when playing bingo?

2. Which city was connected to London by the Flying Scotsman railway service?

3. Which American city is also the title of a 2002 Oscar-winning film starring Catherine Zeta-Jones and Richard Gere?

4. What is usually split in the ratio of 52 white to 36 black?

5. Which children's card game shares its name with one of the mascots of Kellogg's Rice Krispies?

6. 'Oh my God, they killed Kenny' is a line frequently heard in which adult animated TV show?

7. Which female vocalist had one of her first hits, 'Don't Speak', with the band No Doubt?

8. Which word follows 'Al' in the name of a TV news station broadcasting from Doha, Qatar?

9. Which is the only English word that sounds exactly the same if you remove the last four letters from it?

10. A leveret is the name for the young of which animal?

11. Which American actor's big screen roles include Rick Deckard, Richard Kimble, Henry Jones Jr and Jack Ryan?

12. With which field event in athletics would you associate Jan Zelezny?

13. What attribute, according to Thomas Edison, is 1 per cent inspiration and 99 per cent perspiration?

14. Which Middle Eastern city is shown as being at the centre of the world on the medieval 'Mappa Mundi' housed in Hereford Cathedral?

15. Which city was the capital of Spain under the Romans? Now a World Heritage Site, it is also famous for sword-making.

16. The island of Taiwan was historically known by what name, meaning 'beautiful' in Portuguese?

17. At what time did the gunfights take place in the Old West town of Hadleyville? (Two-word answer.)

18. In the late 1960s children's animated TV series *The Herbs*, what kind of animal was Parsley?

19. With atomic number 28, which chemical element comes between cobalt and copper in the periodic table?

20. Which river, for part of its length, forms the boundary between the cities of Manchester and Salford?

21. Which bacteria-based edible product has a name that comes from the Esperanto word for yogurt?

22. Which cyclist is nicknamed 'The Manx Missile'?

23. Which song was a 1959 hit for The Coasters, a 1964 hit for The Paramounts and a 1980 hit for The Lambrettas?

24. What name is given to the variety of pasta resembling a butterfly or bow-tie?

25. The Toy Dolls had a number four hit in 1984 singing about whose departure from the circus?

26. In *Friends*, what is the name of Phoebe's twin sister?

27. Chile shares land borders with Argentina, Bolivia and which other country?

28. How many books are there in C S Lewis's *Narnia* series?

29. Which 17-day-long event begins every September on the Theresienwiese (or St Teresa's Meadow) in Munich?

30. Holly Maddison, Kendra Wilkinson and Bridget Marquardt all starred in which noughties reality television show following their lives in the Playboy mansion?

GENERAL KNOWLEDGE: TOUGH

GENERAL KNOWLEDGE 11

1. Debuting in 1967, which musical had the subtitle 'The American Tribal Love-Rock Musical'?

2. The internet is used by members of the public. What similar name is given to a closed system that might only be used by a specific company or organization?

3. Following his death, Hugh Hefner was buried next to which actress, his first-ever centrefold?

4. The Jones Act of 1917 granted people from which island US citizenship?

5. What is the opposite of dextral (on the right-hand side)?

6. What colour does the prefix 'xantho' indicate?

7. With the atomic number 43, what is the lightest-known element that has no stable isotopes?

8. What name is given to the volcanic glass that is produced when felsic lava extruded from a volcano cools rapidly with minimal crystal growth?

9. Complete the title of this book by Colombian author Gabriel García Márquez – *Love in the Time of…*?

10. Supposedly born on 1 July 1899, which archaeology professor is known, not by his birth name, but by the name his father gave to their family dog?

11. Five days either way, how many days are there in a year on Venus?

12. Who is the only actor to have Emmy nominations for the same part in three different shows?

13. Which room in a house takes its name from the French word for sulking?

14. Which animal nickname has been used to describe motorcyclist Valentino Rossi, sprinter Usain Bolt and boxer Muhammed Ali?

15. Eggbutt snaffle, Pelham, Kimblewick and three-ring Dutch gag are all types of what?

16. Which fictional character has a wonderfully named girlfriend called Piella Bakewell?

17. What do you fear if you are algophobic?

18. Which phrase, meaning to be in a state of anxious suspense, derives from the practice of stretching woollen cloth over a frame to prevent shrinkage?

19. In 1999, which product was blamed for a girl's skin turning orange? It was due to her over-consumption and the amount of beta-carotene colouring in the ingredients.

20. Opened in 1917 and serving as the main hub of the city until 1974 (when a larger airport was opened), Love Field Airport is in which US city?

21. *Nessiteras rhombopteryx* is the scientific name for which aquatic creature?

22. Lys Assia was the first winner of which contest in 1956?

23. Just based on the values of the letters, which European capital city would score the most points in a game of Scrabble – a total of 30?

24. What vegetable was the first product advertised in colour on British TV?

25. The Hundred Years War started in which century?

26. What was deemed to be a crime until 1961 under UK law? If it was done correctly, it would be impossible to issue a punishment for this act.

27. Which member of the Monty Python team called his 2011 tour 'The Alimony Tour', as he used the proceeds from it to pay for his divorce?

28. Meatlinc and Zwartbles are breeds of which farm animal?

29. Which much sought-after type of honey comes from the New Zealand tea tree?

30. Ozone is mainly found in which layer of the earth's atmosphere?

GENERAL KNOWLEDGE 12

1. What was the subtitle of the first film in the *Pirates of the Caribbean* film series?

2. Which 1971 Rod Stewart hit could be linked to two 'unique' British Prime Ministers?

3. What is the unusual physical feature of the Norse god Tyr, after whom Tuesday is named?

4. Anton Chekhov's play *The Three Sisters* is said to have been inspired by which real-life siblings?

5. Who was the author of the book *The Naked Ape*? Published in 1967, it compared humans to other animal species.

6. In which 'sport' do the fouls include blagging, blatching, burting, cobbing and haversacking?

7. When Barbra Streisand won the Best Actress Oscar, she was a joint winner with which other actress?

8. Which Australian location takes its name from the Latin for 'no trees', as no trees grow there?

9. In Egyptian mythology, which goddess has the head of a cat?

10. Nine players under the age of seventeen have played Test cricket. Six of these have played for which country?

11. Deriving its name from the Urdu for 'water monster' and predominantly found in India, what type of creature is a mugger?

12. Based on a play by Pushkin, which Mussorgsky opera is named for a ruler who reigned as tsar from 1598 to 1605?

13. Eglantyne Jebb founded which international charitable organization in 1919?

14. The highest permanently occupied settlement is called La Rinconada and is 5,100m (16,732ft) above sea level. It is in which South American country?

15. Which sportsperson is married to Oscar-winning writer and director Dustin Lance Black?

16. In her five minutes of internet fame, Rebecca Black sang a song about which day of the week?

17. Murdered by the Krays in 1967, Jack 'the Hat' McVitie was so named as he commonly wore what type of hat?

18. Famously portrayed on screen by Woody Harrelson, which US pornography mogul once offered a $10 million incentive for anyone who would provide information that would see Donald Trump get impeached?

19. Barbara Bach, the wife of Ringo Starr, played Bond girl Anya Amasova in which 1977 film?

20. What was notable about Tipperary Tim's victory in the 1928 Grand National?

21. Typing which word into Wikipedia returns the message 'Not to be confused with Cardassian (*Star Trek*)'?

22. What name links the winner of the Best Picture Oscar in 2006 and a 1988 number five hit for The Primitives?

23. According to Jewish folklore, what was the name of Adam's first wife?

24. He was born on board the ship *Ann* off the coast of Port Morant, Jamaica, however his name is synonymous with an island nation over 17,000km (11,000 miles) from his place of birth – who is the British statesman?

25. Collectively, what are Alnitak, Alnilam and Mintaka better known as?

26. Which is the most popular surname in France? In the UK, it would more commonly be a first name.

27. Which French leader is the intended assassination victim in the book *The Day of the Jackal*?

28. Which airport is situated around 210km (130 miles) north of St John's, Newfoundland?

29. The Red River is a tributary of which US river?

30. Which book by Lynne Truss is described as 'the zero tolerance approach to punctuation'?

GENERAL KNOWLEDGE 13

1. Which was the first *Mr. Men* book to be published in 1971?

2. What do you call someone who makes barrels?

3. What number is between 3 and 2 on a dartboard?

4. Watts, joules per second and ergs per second are units used to measure what?

5. In Nintendo games, the character Link is often given the task of finding and rescuing which princess?

6. What name was given to the fortified positions hastily built along the south coast of Britain when Napoleon was gathering a fleet to invade?

7. The po'boy is a traditional type of submarine sandwich originating in which American state?

8. Who said in 1999: 'Marilyn Manson? Yeah, really original. Stick some make-up on and give yourself a girl's name. That's never been done.'?

9. On Japanese TV or in print media, people are legally required to have their hands pixelated if they are wearing what?

10. Gerlachovka is the highest peak in which mountain range?

11. Which company had its HQ at 3 Midland Road, Worcester, WR5 1DT?

12. The *Geococcyx* is a member of the cuckoo family. What name is it better known by?

13. Which legendary American served as a member of the US House of Representatives from 1827 to 1831 representing Tennessee's 9th District and from 1833 to 1835 representing Tennessee's 12th District?

14. Royce Gracie defeated Gerard Gordeau in the first of which type of event in 1993? It was held at the McNichols Sports Arena in Colorado.

15. Pubs called The White Hart were named in honour of which English king?

16. What was the name of the far-left German terrorist gang responsible for more than 30 murders in the 1970s and 1980s?

17. Which BBC sitcom parodied the 1970s wartime drama *Secret Army?*

18. The bright green Dutch liqueur Pisang Ambon is flavoured with which fruit?

19. Better known for his part in another soap, who played Cliff Leyton in *Crossroads?*

20. Which American novel, published in 1852, was subtitled *Life Among the Lowly?*

21. The 1949 treaty of Washington was the basis for the foundation of what?

22. New Zealand-born A J Hackett is the entrepreneur credited with the creation of which extreme activity?

23. *The Epic of Gilgamesh, Hamlet, Much Ado About Nothing* and *Tao Te Ching* are the only four known works to have been translated into which language?

24. From the middle of the 1980s until his death in 1995, which noted medical researcher and virologist spent the final ten years of his life unsuccessfully looking for a cure for HIV and AIDS?

25. What did George Holliday infamously capture on videotape on 3 March 1991 in Los Angeles?

26. Who was commissioned by King Minos of Crete to design the Labyrinth on the island of Crete that housed the Minotaur?

27. In the title of an 1880s American novel, what are the two main characters, Edward Tudor and Tom Canty, known as?

28. The state of Louisiana was named in honour of which French king?

29. The Hawaiian alphabet contains the five vowels and how many consonants?

30. Which group of flatfish is also known as Tonguefishes?

GENERAL KNOWLEDGE 14

1. Which popular cat name means 'happy' or 'lucky 'in Latin?

2. What surname links Graham and Damon – father and son Formula One Champions?

3. In 1967 Charles de Gaulle became the first French leader to make an official visit to which nation, of which he was the joint ruler?

4. In which 1987 film does Jack Nicholson play the devil?

5. The Tynwald is the independent parliament of which part of the British Isles?

6. How did a performance of the play *Our American Cousin* by the English dramatist Tom Taylor find its way into the history books in April 1865?

7. The headlands of the Great Orme and Little Orme are situated close to which Welsh seaside town?

8. Which detective was the most famous creation of crime writer Colin Dexter?

9. Who was Noel Gallagher talking about when he said: 'He's the angriest man you'll ever meet. He's like a man with a fork in a world of soup'?

10. Signed in 1840, the Treaty of Waitangi established British rule over which country?

11. Discovered in 2016 in Papua New Guinea, a new kind of particularly hairy beetle was named after which sci-fi character from the planet Kashyyyk?

12. What name is singer Jake Edwin Charles Kennedy more commonly known by?

13. Which nationally owned company is based in Llantrisant in South Wales?

14. Whose biggest UK hits included 'Wichita Lineman', 'It's Only Make Believe' and 'Rhinestone Cowboy'?

15. Who had the vital statistics 19-19-19?

16. Which UK coastal resort shares its name with the capital of the island of Tobago?

17. Which 'biblical' band had hits with 'Abacab' and 'Mama' in the 1980s?

18. On which island can you find Vicarstown in the east, Kirk Ronan in the south, Harwick in the north and the main towns of Tidmouth and Knapford in the west?

19. About which company did Warren Buffett say: 'I like a business where customers tattoo your name on their chest'?

20. Seeing both main characters joining the army, 'Goodbye to All That' was (in 1966) the final episode of which sitcom?

21. The painting *The Haywain* by Constable depicts a cart crossing which river?

22. When ESPN named their greatest 100 North American athletes of the 20th century, what was the unique link between positions 35 and 84?

23. The inventor of Liquid Paper correction fluid was the mother of which member of The Monkees?

24. If you threw one dart into every scoring segment of a standard dart board, how many points would you score?

25. Which is the only film adapted from a Stephen King novel to have won an Oscar?

26. What anachronism can you find on the US uniforms in the film *Chariots of Fire*?

27. What links Scotchgard, LSD, penicillin, saccharine, X-rays and Post-it Notes?

28. What kind of light has a wavelength of between 400 nanometres and 100 nanometres?

29. With the symbol Sb, which is the first element mentioned by Tom Lehrer in his song 'The Elements'?

30. Also known as the cachalot, what 60-tonne marine creature has the largest brain of any animal? It weighs approximately 8kg (18lb).

GENERAL KNOWLEDGE 15

1. Who had a 1978 hit with 'Love Is in the Air'?

2. Which internet search engine was set up by David Filo and Jerry Yang in 1994?

3. What took place at Max Yasgur's farm from 15 to 18 August 1969?

4. Which European capital city is on the River Tagus?

5. In *The Simpsons*, what is the name of Chief Wiggum's son?

6. With which type of films would you most associate the late George A Romero?

7. The Spanish alphabet contains 27 letters. Which letter is repeated, with the addition of a tilde?

8. Which self-described 'stately homo of Britain' once said: 'When I told the people of Northern Ireland that I was an atheist, a woman in the audience stood up and said: "Yes, but is it the God of the Catholics or the God of the Protestants in whom you don't believe?"'?

9. What is the name of Dr Doolittle's talking parrot?

10. In September 1980, who said: 'Recession is when your neighbour loses his job. Depression is when you lose yours'?

11. Balsamic vinegar is associated with which Italian province?

12. Which *Lord of the Rings* actor played the title character in the universally panned 1994 film *North*?

13. In 1774, Captain James Cook named which island nation New Hebrides? This name would last until the country gained its independence in 1980.

14. Published in 1950, a paper entitled 'Computing Machinery and Intelligence' was the first to suggest which test, named after the author of the paper?

15. Which James Bond film saw former WWE wrestler Dave Bautista playing an assassin called Mr Hinx?

16. In 2005, George Galloway was elected as MP for Bethnal Green and Bow while standing as a candidate for which party?

17. Played by Andrew Robinson, the murderous villain in the film *Dirty Harry* was known by what nickname?

18. What is the most commonly spoken language of South Africa? Over 11 million people use it as a first language.

19. Mario Cavaradossi, Baron Scarpia and Cesare Angelotti are characters in which Puccini opera?

20. What was the real surname of Fats Domino, one of the pioneers of rock and roll?

21. What name is given to a lift that consists of a chain of open compartments moving continuously in a loop?

22. What specific compass point would be found at 247.5 degrees clockwise from north?

23. The name of which African capital city is 11 letters long and made up of 8 vowels and 3 consonants?

24. In Shakespeare's 18th sonnet, which eight words precede 'Thou art more lovely and more temperate'?

25. Trichology is the medical study of which part of the body?

26. Which song from the film *South Pacific* topped the UK singles chart in 1982?

27. Who had a cameo role as a waitress in the 2000 Julia Roberts film *Erin Brockovich*?

28. In which sport can you score one point for 'a behind'?

29. Which is the only US state to permit its residents to cast absentee ballots from space?

30. Sharing its name with a Glenda Jackson film, what is the name of the first episode of *Fawlty Towers*, shown in 1975?

GENERAL KNOWLEDGE: BRUTAL

GENERAL KNOWLEDGE 16

1. The leg on the poster for the film *The Graduate* belongs to which actress, more famous for her role in *Dallas*?

2. Which is the only breed of penguin to inhabit the northern hemisphere?

3. The name of which place, highly prominent in November remembrance, means 'empty tomb'?

4. Sam Allardyce played league football for nine different teams. Which was the only club he represented more than a hundred times?

5. Born in 1518, the painter Jacopo Comin was more commonly known by what name?

6. Which English author gives his name to a type of omelette incorporating smoked haddock, Parmesan cheese and cream?

7. Named after one of the first people in the UK to die from AIDS, which British charity is Europe's largest HIV/AIDS charity?

8. We all know that K2 is the second-highest mountain in the world, but which mountain in Pakistan was originally known as K1?

9. Located in Bergen and now functioning as a museum, Troldhaugen is the former home of which composer, who lived from 1843 to 1907?

10. In 2016, which British cyclist became the first Summer Olympic gold medallist to compete in the 24 Hours of Le Mans?

11. Around half of all the TV sets manufactured in Europe are produced by Beko and Vestel. In which country are both companies headquartered?

12. Which historically important 9-hectare (22-acre) area is named after the California brown pelicans that lived there in huge numbers during the 18th and 19th centuries?

13. After dwindling sales of its normal products and filing for bankruptcy in 2012, which large US company launched its first smartphone, the IM5, in 2015?

14. Rick Dees & His Cast of Idiots sang about what kind of bird? (Two-word answer.)

15. Which pirate lost his most famous ship, *The Queen Anne's Revenge*, while attempting to blockade the port of Beaufort Inlet, North Carolina, in 1718?

16. Which site in County Durham is called 'The Living Museum of the North'?

17. Which type of car takes its name from a collective group of clans that originate in Iran and Eastern Turkey?

18. Who directed the films *The Wild Bunch*, *Major Dundee* and *Bring Me the Head of Alfredo Garcia*?

19. Released in 1999, what was the final video game console made by Sega?

20. In which sport is the Commissioner's Trophy awarded?

21. Which South American city was the destination of Air France's maiden Concorde flight in 1976?

22. Apparently, according to the book of Leviticus, you cannot wear clothes that are made from more than how many types of fabric?

23. Which country is host to the annual World 'Wife-carrying' Championship? First prize is the wife's weight in beer.

24. Whose first act as US President was to pardon people who had avoided the draft for the Vietnam War?

25. What links bunny wars, monkey's fist, lark's head and daisy chain?

26. What animated film was released in Israel with the title *Rain of Falafel?*

27. What do people suffering from trichotillomania have a compulsion to do?

28. How old was Hitler when he died?

29. Which unit of the Roman army consisted of approximately 480 men?

30. Which footwear is also a venomous snake?

GENERAL KNOWLEDGE 17

1. In which 1980 film would you find Bob's Country Bunker, where they have both kinds of music, Country AND Western?

2. Who played the Absinthe Fairy in the film *Moulin Rouge?*

3. In the Bible, what is the name of Cain's first-born son?

4. Vincent van Gogh was born in Zundert, Netherlands, in 1853, but died in which country?

5. What first did Norwell Roberts achieve by being accepted into the Metropolitan Police in April 1967?

6. As featured in a 1987 film set in 2017, what is the name of the television game show hosted by Damon Killian?

7. Which site in South Carolina was the location of the first battle of the American Civil War?

8. Which electronic music group, formed in Berlin in 1967 by Edgar Froese, composed the original score for the video game *Grand Theft Auto V?*

9. Which word is used to describe the scattering of races – particularly Jews – throughout the world?

10. In 1983, Thomas Dolby had a minor hit with a song called 'She Blinded Me with Science'. The accompanying video featured a cameo appearance by a then very well-known TV scientist/personality. Who was he?

11. Which British luxury car manufacturer was founded in Cricklewood, north London, in 1919 and has been owned by Volkswagen since 1998?

12. Which brewery in Witney, Oxfordshire, produces Piledriver beer, named after a Status Quo album?

13. Who was the Jamaican nurse who set up the British Hotel during the Crimean War and in a 2004 poll was voted the greatest Black Briton?

14. The traditional Royal Navy game of Uckers, invented in the late 18th century, was an early version of which now popular board game?

15. Stretching a total of 425km (264 miles), which is New Zealand's longest river?

16. In jazz music, which instrument was Errol Garner most famous for playing?

17. The parks and palaces of Sans Souci, the largest World Heritage Site in Germany, are located in which city, the capital of the Brandenburg State?

18. At her wedding, Princess Eugenie's dress revealed a long scar down her back, from an operation to cure which affliction when she was younger?

19. Actor Terence Stamp played which role in the original *Superman* film series?

20. Which composer, born in 1854, wrote the opera *Hansel and Gretel?* His name is now more commonly associated with popular music.

21. How many players are there on a hurling team?

22. Which African country is the most populous landlocked country in the world?

23. Which creature appears on the logo of the website Tripadvisor?

24. Minoru Yamasaki in 1972 and 1973, and David Childs in November 2014. What is the architectural connection?

25. What type of sausage derives its name from the Italian word for 'onion'?

26. Which Canadian-born actress is best known for playing Lois Lane opposite Christopher Reeve's Superman?

27. Edward 'Monks' Leeford is the half-brother of which Dickens character?

28. What Italian name is given to the kitchen implement consisting of a crescent-shaped, two-handled blade, commonly used to chop herbs?

29. What two-word sociology term describes a politically unstable country whose economy is largely dependent on the export of a single product, such as fruits or minerals?

30. Which American poet (1885–1972) wrote 'Ripostes', 'Hugh Selwyn Mauberley' and the 120-section collection *The Cantos*?

GENERAL KNOWLEDGE 18

1. On which popular TV quiz show were Greek letters replaced by Egyptian hieroglyphs at the start of season 4?

2. What is the real first name of legendary cricket umpire 'Dickie' Bird?

3. What began in 1848 after a discovery by James W Marshall in Sutter's Mill?

4. At which Winter Olympics did Eddie 'the Eagle' Edwards famously finish last in both ski jumping events?

5. Which horse race was first run in 1780, the first winner being Diomed?

6. As well as John Paul I, which other pope died in 1978?

7. In which Scottish town is Ross County's football ground?

8. Perhaps the best known of all Greek vocalists, Demis Roussos was actually born in which African country?

9. The name of which beer completes this line from a Monty Python sketch featuring 'mindless oafs squirting Timothy White's sun cream over their puffy raw, swollen flesh' after 'stopping at Majorcan bodegas selling fish and chips and…'?

10. 'Bamboo' is a perfume released by which fashion house?

11. Name the ship that survived Pearl Harbor but was sunk in 1982.

12. What is or was a demi-culverin?

13. Which comic actor who died of an overdose in 1988 wrote 'Oh, what's the bloody point?' as the final entry in his diary?

14. Actor Dustin Diamond played the annoying character of Screech Powers in which teen TV series?

15. Born in Liverpool in 1960, which singer (the frontman of a successful band) was long believed to have been born in Sudan – a lie he told in an interview for a music magazine?

16. *The Singing Butler* and *Mad Dogs*, both featuring a beach and umbrellas, are among the works of which British artist?

17. What is the name of the eatery in Coney Island, New York, that plays host to the annual 4 July hot-dog eating competition, won frequently by Joey Chestnut?

18. What is the name of the musician and journalist who appeared as a panellist on *That's Life* from 1989 to 1992 and who, under the pseudonym Ivor Biggun, has released four albums of smutty songs?

19. What is the name of the Englishman whose grave in Westminster Abbey claims he lived for 152 years, during the reign of 10 monarchs? He was reportedly born in 1483 and died in 1635.

20. Which tree usually provides the wood used to make Highland Games cabers?

21. Which word for 'disinformation' comes from the Latin for 'preaching the faith'?

22. The French TGV rail service opened to the public in 1981 with services running between Paris and which other French city?

23. Founded in 1703 in Barbados, what is the world's oldest rum distillery?

24. In the *Peanuts* cartoon strip, what is the surname of Lucy and her younger brothers Linus and Rerun?

25. At what age did both Princess Diana and Marilyn Monroe die?

26. Which is Britain's largest National Park by area?

27. Which famous person is credited with making platinum a popular metal for jewellery in the 1940s?

28. What was the name of the notorious assassination squad, also known as the Brownsville Boys, that was headed by gangster Albert Anastasia?

29. Who said: 'She got her looks from her father – he's a plastic surgeon'?

30. 'All Time High' by Rita Coolidge is the theme tune to which James Bond film?

GENERAL KNOWLEDGE 19

1. In 1787, William Herschel discovered Titania and Oberon, moons of which planet?

2. In *Around the World in 80 Days*, Phileas Fogg starts and ends his circumnavigation at which London club?

3. Which system of waterfalls on the Argentina-Brazil border was named in 2007 as one of the Seven New Wonders of Nature?

4. For what reason would people in the 19th and early 20th centuries refer to a *Bradshaw*?

5. Mix a sextarius of water with 9 ounces of honey. The whole is exposed to the sun for 40 days, and then left on a shelf near the fire. If you have no rain water, then boil spring water. This is an ancient recipe for which drink?

6. Which former political leader set out his 'Third Universal Theory of Governing' in his so-called 'Little Green Book'?

7. What is the name of the fictional island that is home to the Jurassic Park complex?

8. Terry Yorath managed the national teams of two countries. Wales was one, which country was the other?

9. What name is given to a post or target mounted on a pole to be tilted at as jousting practice by knights?

10. Sharing its name with an Antarctic volcano, what name is given to the primordial Greek deity that personified darkness?

11. Which Chinese strategy board game is usually played on a grid of 19 x 19 squares?

12. Who provided the voice of Mufasa, father of Simba in the Disney film *The Lion King*?

13. How are Drizella and Anastasia Tremaine known collectively?

14. Fictional characters Clint Barton, Benjamin Pierce and Natty Bumppo all share which nickname?

15. Which goddess was the wife of the Norse god Odin?

16. Which of the great apes belongs to a sub-family called Pongo?

17. Who was the Austrian musicologist (1800–1877) who is best known for cataloguing the works of Mozart and originating the 'K-numbers' by which they are known?

18. The 2010 animated film *Tangled* was a retelling of which classic fairy tale?

19. In which holy book does it state that there are 19 angels guarding Hell?

20. Differing from the name of another letter by just one letter, what is the twentieth letter of the Greek alphabet?

21. Which footballer appeared on *Desert Island Discs* as the show celebrated its 75th anniversary?

22. Which future Oscar-winning actor was the room-mate of future US Vice President Al Gore when they studied together at Harvard?

23. What name is shared by a brand of Volkswagen car and a cocker spaniel that was owned by the Duke and Duchess of Cambridge?

24. In the Tour de France, what is indicated by the flamme rouge?

25. In which US state is the vast majority of Yellowstone National Park?

26. Which lover of chewing gum was last seen being escorted to the juicing room where it was hoped that she could be returned to her normal size and colour?

27. The BABE car rally runs from the Big Apple New York to which other major US city?

28. What will you suffer if you have sphenopalatine ganglioneuralgia?

29. The controversial 'Zimmermann Telegram' sent by the German Foreign Office in 1917 encouraged which country to declare war on the USA in return for the land that they claimed during an invasion?

30. *The Simpsons* was first seen in 1987 as a portion of whose US TV show?

GENERAL KNOWLEDGE 20

1. Which Australian Prime Minister is presumed to have drowned while swimming at Portsea, near Melbourne, on 17 December 1967?

2. What name is shared by the real-life fourth Governor of New Hampshire and a fictional Governor of New Hampshire who would later become President of the USA?

3. Although he didn't take part in the fighting himself, Alfred H Terry was in overall command of the US Army at which battle that took place on 25–26 June 1876?

4. Which British TV series, that ran from 2007 to 2011, starred Andrew-Lee Potts and Hannah Spearritt who encounter various dinosaurs that appear on Earth via temporal anomalies?

5. Better known now in the field of beverages, who was Prime Minister of the UK from 1830 to 1834?

6. Which Derbyshire farmer is credited with inventing the concept of 'Pick Your Own' when he invited people onto his farm to collect strawberries in the early 1960s? He would later become a household name on TV and radio.

7. Three to five separate or fused vertebrae, situated below the sacrum, are collectively known by what name?

8. A 1774 review of the laws of cricket introduced which method of dismissal?

9. What name is given to the seventh Sunday after Easter, which commemorates the descent of the Holy Spirit on the Apostles?

10. Humberto Delgado Airport serves which European city?

11. In times of Indian colonialism, which Hindi word was used as a polite form of address for European women?

12. What board game was the first to have a computer world champion?

13. Which year of the 20th century saw the first appearance of Halley's Comet?

14. In the *Discworld* novels of Terry Pratchett, what is the bizarre name of the conman postmaster of Ankh Morpork Post Office?

15. Beaujolais nouveau wines are made entirely from which wine grape?

16. Samsung, Hyundai and LG are examples of which large South Korean business groups that dominate that economy?

17. What name is given to the first of the month in the Roman calendar?

18. Hives and nettle rash are alternative names for which skin condition?

19. Which actor played the father of Benjamin Braddock in *The Graduate?* His crowning glory must surely be voicing the supercar KITT in *Knight Rider*.

20. CQR, Danforth and mushroom are types of what?

21. What style of hat is also the name of a character who appeared in the Channel 4 sitcom *Desmond's*?

22. Which African country shares its name with the small piece of paper which is popped out by a hole-punch?

23. Which Olympic track event has the longest-standing world record? (Distance and gender required.)

24. Cindy Breakspeare was crowned Miss World in 1976. She is however arguably more famous for her relationship with which musical legend in the late 1970s?

25. Jamaican political leader Marcus Garvey died in 1940 after suffering a stroke. His stroke is attributed to the fact that he was in major shock after reading whose obituary in the *Chicago Defender* newspaper?

26. Which album by Fairport Convention shares its name with a popular instant pudding?

27. Tamworth, Mangalitza and Duroc are types of which animal?

28. The crime novels of which author include *Sanitarium of Death*, *The Dead Man Sang* and *The Venomous Valentine*?

29. Whose portrait is the most famous work of artist Basil Hallward?

30. Which word can be used as a prefix to both 'smock' and 'tresses' to provide the names of two flowering plants?

THE BEAST'S
TIPS & TRICKS

There is no magic trick to becoming a good quizzer. You can't press a button and say: 'I want to be a great quizzer' and then a week later receive a certificate telling you that you are. Why? Because, by definition, general knowledge is huge and to know as much as you can, you have to soak up a lot of information at all times and work out which of it is worth knowing. Being a good quizzer has to come from within – you've really got to want to do it.

HOW TO ACQUIRE AND STORE INFORMATION

One of the things I do is read a good-quality newspaper every day. As I'm looking through it, I think: 'Is this something I'm going to need to know in the future?' In other words, you read a story and ask yourself: 'Has it got legs? Are people going to care about this in a month's time?' When I was a question writer, I was forever scanning the papers spotting interesting little factlets and filing them away. For example, if someone wins a country's first-ever gold medal, then that will be worth remembering. I know who won the bronze medal in rowing at the 2004 Athens Olympics in the quad scull, but I would never expect to see that question appear in a general knowledge quiz because it's a bronze medal that was won in a year when Great Britain won a load more gold medals. There's nothing distinctive about it. By contrast, when Fiji won their first-ever Olympic gold medal in the rugby sevens, I'd argue that's a bigger deal because of its historical context. Chris Hoy winning his three gold medals at the 2008 Beijing Olympics also made a big impact and is a great general knowledge question.

I generally store all this information in my head. A lot of people note things down in notebooks but the modern digital equivalent is online flashcards, and it's the method that younger quizzers – especially American ones – swear by. So you write the information down and store it away, and then you get the machine to randomly ask you questions. Hmm, that's not for me. I don't want to sound like a dinosaur, but I'll stick to my own tried and tested methods because I'm 56. But we will all have our own methods of remembering stuff, so go with whichever one works for you.

Paul Sinha puts in around ten or twelve hours a day of research with his husband and, to be fair, he's a better quizzer than me. But in contrast, I don't swot – I just top up everything I need to know by watching something like *Downton Abbey*. Sitting in front of the telly might not sound like work, but we get asked so many questions about shows like that. I will watch a couple of episodes of any TV show that has a bit of a buzz around it, gauge what it's about and see who the key characters are and who plays them, because I know that they are likely to come up as key questions. When I go to see films like *Top Gun: Maverick*, I pay attention because I can imagine being asked questions about it. It's a big film. While I'm watching, I'm filing away all the little things I read or see, trying to work out if it could be a question in an upcoming game.

But I would say the best way of taking things in is when you actually enjoy what you are researching. Someone once said about

Kevin Ashman from *Eggheads*, who in my mind is one of the greatest quizzers who have ever lived, that 'he never met a museum he didn't love'. He's just interested in everything and easily takes it in. And that is the key. Apparently, every morning he gets out a green highlighter and enthusiastically highlights anything he reads that he thinks might be useful in the future. You've got to admire that kind of preparation. But while Kevin is great at soaking up information, he has admitted that there is one subject that he's terrible at mastering – horse-racing. Why? Because he has no interest in it whatsoever. He says he's tried to work up an interest but just can't. I agree with that. If you're interested in something, it will go in almost without you realizing it. If you're not interested in it, it's like revising for an exam. And we all know how boring that is.

What I have discovered along the way is that I'm not great at focus learning. If I'm learning something I have to, it doesn't go in nearly as easily as when I'm just casually absorbing information. For example, when I do panto, I find learning my lines quite hard. But, of course, I have to ensure that I say the precise words every time, so that my fellow actors know when to come in.

I did my law degree when I was 30, having worked as a teacher for years. I really enjoyed studying a lot more at that point in my life because I actually wanted to do it and was keen to read up on the subject. We appreciate different things as we get older. What we found boring when we were teenagers at school might be something we become intrigued by in later life – something we will go off and study in detail off our own bat. A teacher friend of mine recently told me that kids always ask: 'What's the point of learning about stuff like algebra that we don't often use in the real world?' I get where they're coming from, but my take on it is, algebra is like the mental equivalent of push-ups. A push-up is useless on its own but what it does do is build up your strength. Algebra helps you think logically. It can help you learn, long after you've left school.

The bottom line though is that everyone is wired in a certain way. Some are creative, while some are better at dealing with facts and figures. When it comes to subjects like English, history and geography, you can see a clear difference between the level of knowledge of 15- or 16-year-olds and 11- or 12-year-olds. Their writing styles will be different. Whereas with maths, a gifted 12-year-old can easily do better than some 16-year-olds will ever do, because their minds just aren't set up that way, no matter how hard they work. It's like sport, where the rules are set up to make things as fair as possible but some people will have a huge natural advantage based on genetics and what God gave them. If I had been 5 foot 7, I would never have been picked to be on my basketball team but, at 6 foot 6, they wanted me. A writer for *Sports Illustrated* once claimed that, based on available statistics, if you're 7 foot tall in the United States, there is a one in six chance of you playing for the National Basketball Association league at some point. It's one of the most competitive sports in the world, but by the simple fact of being 7 foot tall, someone has a sporting chance of playing top-level basketball.

I have the academic equivalent. You don't realize you have it at first.

PREPARING FOR THE CHASE

When it comes to preparing for the show, I just do what I always do – read up on what's going on. There are certain subjects like sport, science, history and geography that I'm fairly confident with, so I will focus on ever-changing areas like current affairs, maybe children's literature, food and drink and entertainment, though I'm still not very good on soaps generally. Recently on *The Chase*, I've noticed quite a few questions about the road and motorway systems. My fellow Chasers usually get stumped by these, but as I drive a lot it's the kind of question that I enjoy. You can prepare all you like, but you never know what's going to catch you.

Becoming a Chaser is a whole different kettle of fish than becoming a good quizzer. Over the years I have had so many people ask me about it, because basically they want to get on TV in what they see as an academic version of *Love Island*. They'll have that glossy telegenic look that producers adore, but then they'll turn around and ask me: 'When do they give you the answers?' I'll tell them: 'They don't.' And they look at me in horror. I hope the show's producers never go down that road because you'd never see the likes of Anne, who was the best female quizzer in the world a few years back; you wouldn't see Paul, Britain's champion; or Shaun, *Mastermind* champion; or me, multiple pub competition champion. None of us would make it onto the show. Let's face it, they'd have much better-looking actors doing the jobs.

There are many young people who are becoming interested in quizzing and building up their skills playing online games. I think one day soon there'll be quizzers in their thirties, maybe mid-twenties, who are easily good enough to be Chasers. The downside is these guys have acquired their info in a dark room surfing the net, so they might not have the social skills to be a Chaser on the telly yet.

MODERN QUIZZING

Once upon a time it was easy – or at least, easier – to be a quizzer because the means of seeking information was much more limited than it is today. Paul Sinha says he wishes he'd started quizzing when the Internet was what it is now, as it would have made a huge difference. There is so much information available to you. But I think perhaps there's too much, which makes it much harder to know what is necessary to remember or for quizzing to continue in the same way.

Forty years ago, there were fewer TV channels, so by default more of us would see the same shows. Those were the halcyon days when shows were watched by ten, fifteen, twenty million people, whereas these days, three or four million is considered a great number. A large proportion of the young population doesn't watch terrestrial television, they go straight to YouTube or streaming services like Netflix and Amazon. It's there you find loads of brilliantly made science fiction or historical dramas that most people might not see. Searching through Netflix recently, I was both surprised and shocked to see dozens of swords and sorcery shows – it's the kind of thing I like, but I had never heard of any of them. And if I haven't, then neither have many other people like me. There's just too much choice to be had. How on earth are we supposed to know what is being watched by the majority? How are quizmasters to know what questions will appeal to most of their quizzers?

I'm going to sound like an old fart by saying this, but this fascination with streaming, YouTube and TikTok will inevitably lead – if it's not happening already – to a big change in quizzing. The entertainment world has now become so much more fractured that it's going to be really hard to keep track of everything. Which is tough on an old quizzer like me. This could mean that the art of quizzing may become more fragmented and quiz questions could be geared towards certain kinds of people who have certain parameters of knowledge.

I would say the best quizzes are the ones that feature questions that all kinds of people should know the answers to, whether they picked them up from the media or from reading or from school. The late, great *University Challenge* presenter Bamber Gascoigne described general knowledge quizzes best: 'When you hear the answer, you feel you should have known it.' Which makes perfect sense. If you come away from a quiz not recognizing anything that has been said, then it's not the quiz for you. I recently did a quiz in which one of the questions was: 'Who scored the winning goal for Real Madrid when they beat Liverpool at the Champions League Final in the summer of 2022?' The only people who would know or even care about that answer would be a high-level sports quiz team. I was also asked recently which female vocalist had come out of retirement after seven years to record her sixth studio album – and unless you've seen this particular news story, there's nothing to hang your hat on here. There's no clue within the question to help steer you in the right direction. This story was not big enough news for a question in a general knowledge quiz.

Quizzing is not like poker where anyone can have a good day at a given time. It's more like snooker, in that you know before you start playing that if you're up against someone good, you're probably going to lose. When I played the circuit, regularly seeing the same faces, I could pretty much guarantee I was going to come somewhere between about 14th and 20th. It was that predictable. When I was playing well, I'd be seventh, eighth or ninth, because on the grand prix circuit they'd ask a certain level of questions, which tended to be very topical, especially sport. I'd say around half a dozen questions out of 30 would have been about things that had happened within the last year. When I take part in the World Quizzing Championships, which are a bit of a big deal, I tend to score around the 120 mark, while the winning score is about 170. People are always surprised that I'm not scoring higher and ask me why I don't try harder to make up the difference. But they have no idea how much work would be needed to even make an extra ten points. Paul and Anne do, but for me, life is way too short.

But if I did want to do some extra work, I'd focus on the areas that I'm not great at. I don't need to bother with putting any more effort into my strong subjects, like western sports. But I have to accept that the questions at the World Quizzing Championships will have a more international focus because the players are from all around the world. So to prepare, I might read up on Asian cinema, Bollywood and Japanese cinema. Or maybe I'd bone up on the last couple of Indian prime ministers, for example.

ESSENTIAL SUBJECTS YOU SHOULD LEARN

If you love quizzing but want to improve your performance in competition, then there are some essential subjects that you should know about.

US PRESIDENTS

At most points in history, the big man (and, one day, woman) residing in the White House is either the most important person in the world or the second most. In some ways they define their decade so it is more than likely that a question or two on US Presidents will arise from time to time. Which of them should you be aware of? My advice is all of them, but perhaps focus on those in office since World War Two. Of course, it depends on who your quizmaster is. If you're dealing with younger hosts, you might just get away with George W Bush, Barack Obama, Donald Trump and Joe Biden.

But don't just research how many terms they've served – you should also furnish yourself with some associated trivia about them.

For example, Joe Biden is the oldest man to take on the role of President. He is also the President to have received the most votes of any American President in history. Interesting note, the man he kicked out of the Oval Office, Donald Trump, secured the second-most votes of all time. On the subject of Trump, he's often referred to as '45' because a lot of hardcore Democrats couldn't bear to mention his name. He's also the President who won an election despite the fact that his opponent, Hillary Clinton, actually received three million more votes than him in the 2016 presidential race – but that's the American system for you, getting the votes in the right states.

Barack Obama was the first non-white President. He was born in 1961 but, had he been born two years earlier, he would have been ineligible to become President because Hawaii only became a state in 1959 and to be US President you have to be born in the US. That's why at the time of Obama's election, a lot of Republicans were keen to see his passport to confirm that he was actually born in the right place and at the right time. Some years ago, Hollywood actor Arnold Schwarzenegger, who was the 38th governor of California, announced he wanted to run for President. However, because the US constitution states that the President and Vice-President of the country must be natural-born citizens of the United States, be at least 35 years old and have been a resident in the country for at least 14 years, he wasn't eligible. Not that that stopped Arnie. Undeterred, he tried to get the constitutional rules changed so he could run for President in 2016.

If you look at other governmental jobs, like Secretary of State, there is no requirement to have been born in America. Henry Kissinger was born in Germany, while Madeleine Albright was born in what was then Czechoslovakia. For obvious reasons, Secretaries of State often have an international background.

CAPITALS OF THE WORLD – THE GIFT THAT KEEPS ON GIVING

There are two questions people always ask to catch me out. One is about their local football team, which I won't have a clue about, and the other one is what's the capital of a certain country. The latter is a gem and should pose no problem to anyone who has taken some time to learn and memorize them. You see, the beauty of this question is that they rarely change. I can't count the number of times I've had some clever dick thinking they can catch me out by asking what's the capital of Mongolia. And when I reply Ulan Bator they look dumbfounded and stammer: 'What? How did you know that?' The simple answer is I learned them as a kid. I wasn't being a quizzer, I just wanted to know. But knowing the capital cities of the world is essential because you will be asked about them in every general knowledge quiz you do.

Again, don't just learn the names of the cities, try to retain some fun facts about those cities too. For example, Brasilia was designed in the shape of an aeroplane by Oscar Niemeyer. It was one of the first created capitals. Canberra in Australia was basically chosen as capital because both Melbourne and Sydney wanted the gig and they argued about it, so in the end some nowhere place halfway between the two was chosen. And there are the weird and wonderful facts like La Paz in Bolivia being 3,640m (11,942ft) above sea level and not needing a fire brigade because there's not enough oxygen in the air to support combustion. It also means the boiling point of water is lower there, so when you're making a cup of tea you keep an eye on the water as it boils before it is hot enough. Tokyo is an anagram of Japan's previous capital Kyoto. It's one of those questions that keep getting asked because it's a weird little fact that sounds vaguely interesting, so quizmasters tend to include it, not realizing that people have probably heard it half a dozen times in the last four or five years. We get through a hundred thousand questions a year, and while I do love the well-crafted, unusual questions, sometimes it's satisfying to hear the old tried and tested ones: 'What's the capital of…?'

TV AND FILM

As I've mentioned before, when it comes to boning up on my TV knowledge, I basically adopt the 'is there a positive buzz about this show?' approach. It isn't scientific, but it works. A show like *Broadchurch* had a buzz about it, so I watched the first series. *Bodyguard* did as well, so I watched it. *Downton Abbey*, obviously. The shows that are huge hits and get talked about are the ones to focus on. *The Crown* I've watched about four or five episodes of and basically kept a list of who's playing who in it, because questions about it come up time and time again. So watch a handful of episodes and get the gist of the plot and who the main characters are, especially if it's a big-name actor or actress – there's no point in watching the rest. That's all you need to know for quizzing.

My fellow chaser Shaun has trouble with TV questions because for him TV mainly exists for one thing – watching football! And *Frasier*. But how many questions are you going to get on *Frasier*? Not many! You will only ever be asked a few questions about a particular show and they will really be about the three or four main characters or presenters.

With films, I notice that one of the ways you can tell the difference between a quizzer and the average film fan is that quizzers learn about film directors because they're easy to remember. Joe Public won't know who a director is, unless it's Spielberg or Hitchcock or someone like that. In a quiz, you're more likely to be asked who directed a certain film as it's more precise. One lazy question I hear a lot is who starred in a film, and I'll pipe up and say: 'What do you mean, there were three or four main stars in that film.' Then you realize the quiz writer has probably just seen the trailer and mentioned the one person they recognized in it.

I remember being asked: 'When *Star Wars* was first released, which actor got top billing?' To start with you're stuck there thinking who played such and such, what was the starring role – it's interpretive. But in the end the answer was Alec Guinness, which made sense because at the time he was the most famous person in the film. You can know everything about everything but then be blindsided with a badly thought-out question that has most likely been written by someone who's not an expert on the subject because they've just grabbed a fact off the net that they think sounds good.

MUSIC

What I do with music is find a radio station that is playing some mix of contemporary stuff and classics. I mean, I really should listen to Radio 1, but I'm sorry, I'm too old for it – it just does my head in. These days I will listen to a lot of stations and not really know many of the songs or artists. However, I will take note of tracks that are associated with films or TV shows, like Kate Bush's 'Running Up That Hill', which hit the top spot for the first time in 2022, 37 years after it was originally released, after being featured on *Stranger Things*. I will also remember songs that have spent an exceptional time at number one, or hits that feature high-profile collaborations. At the moment, I'm listening to Virgin Radio and Absolute Eighties and Nineties, but I already know most of the songs and facts associated with them. I should really be listening to Absolute Noughties to try and learn some new stuff.

A while back, me and the other Chasers noticed that the producers were asking a lot of questions about contemporary number ones, so over the course of one weekend, one of the Chasers – I won't say who – produced a list of number ones from the 2010s, which we all learned over the weekend. Suddenly we were getting them all right, and the producers were surprised by our fresh knowledge of contemporary music. But that was us noticing a trend with the question writers, of whom there are between six and eight. And we do notice when one of the team has been on holiday to Turkey, for example, because all of a sudden, we get about 20 questions on that country.

KINGS AND QUEENS

Kings and queens of England is another subject to swot up on. Make sure you know that the Tudors were followed by the Stuarts, who were then succeeded by the House of Hanover. Those are actually fundamental. I noticed that on *Are You Smarter Than a 10 Year Old?* they asked a few questions on Scottish monarchs. And maybe it's because I'm old, but I was never taught much about the Scottish monarchs! I guess producers are now trying to be inclusive to the other countries in the British Isles.

Questions about the royals are popular in quizzes, so do read up on as much trivia as you can. Her Majesty is now officially the second-longest reigning monarch in world history. If she gets past 73 years on the throne, she'll have outlasted Louis XIV of France, but he had the advantage of inheriting the throne as a child. Regardless, this is a record that probably won't happen again for many years, definitely not in my lifetime.

Other little bits of trivia may come in handy, like the fact that George VI was a keen sportsman and once played at Wimbledon in the men's doubles. He also served at the Battle of Jutland so he saw active combat. Those of you who like film but are not so *au fait* with the lives of the royals should learn Oscar-winning films about British royalty, a topic that I've encountered at various competitions.

THE CHEMICAL ELEMENTS

The periodic table is one of the most essential subjects to learn – it really is just a case of remembering the letters and what they refer to. It's a great universal type of question, because around the world the elements are the same. 'Fe' always stands for iron, wherever you go. That's a good one to learn, but although there are about 120 elements at the moment, only material scientists and theoretical physicists really need to know all of them – most of us don't. Just focus on the obvious ones, the elements you've heard of. They're more likely to be asked about, rather than something a little more obscure. What's the only three-letter element? Tin. But you probably already knew that. But did you know tin is also known as stannum, and the stanneries are the areas where tin is mined in Cornwall? You might also want to learn the meaning of words, for example that hydrogen comes from *hýdo-r*, the ancient Greek for 'water', or that chlorine is derived from the Greek for 'light green'.

LEARN FROM YOUR MISTAKES

It's all well and good learning facts but I would say, as an old-school quizzer, you can't beat experience. So get out there and quiz, whether it's one at your local pub or a larger event elsewhere. And don't worry if you don't win, or can't answer some of the questions – this is good. Getting questions wrong and learning from them can really help build your confidence and your knowledge. In fact, I think it's the best way of picking up facts that you didn't previously know, so that you can remember them should you be asked about them in another quiz. If you want to take quizzing seriously, then make sure you play with a good quiz team.

When I was playing with my mates Gary Derby and Richie Parnell, I learned so much from them. They were focused, they listened, they learned and they became stronger players because of it. But there have been some folks I have played alongside who have no interest in the game at all, and did not take note of the answers to the questions they got wrong. Then years later I get those same people saying to me: 'Remember when I was on the same quiz team as you? I was as good as you.' And all I can say in response is: 'Er, yeah!' Linford Christie said he used to bump into old school friends who would tell him: 'I used to beat you in races when we were like 12, 13, 14.' And his genius response? 'What happened to you guys, then?' The difference was he kept training and kept working and getting better while the others did other things or life got in the way.

THE DEFAULT ANSWER

If you're faced with a question that you really don't know the answer to, just take an educated guess. There's a whole chunk of good default answers and they roughly go like this: If the question is about fruit, try apple, because there are more varieties than of anything else. If it's about a flower, go with rose, because again there are so many more kinds. If it's an animal you've never heard of, say bird or fish. If it's about a Prime Minister, try Churchill or Thatcher. If it's a witty quote, say Oscar Wilde. If it's about who created such-and-such a word or phrase, try William Shakespeare, because I think he's listed in the dictionary as having created more words in the English language than anybody else. Which country?

Well, what does the name sound like? Does it sound French? If it does, then put down France. This is the one that nearly always works. If it sounds Japanese, put down Japan. People may laugh if your answer is wrong, but I always say it's better to throw up any answer than none. You never know, you might get lucky.

PRACTISE PRACTISE PRACTISE

I'm lucky in that I was born with a great memory, but to be a really good quizzer you have to really practise. You need to do your research and soak up information. Although I can be lazy and won't stretch myself too much, I do make sure for my job that I am fully aware of what is going on in the world so that I am up to date. One of the best ways to improve your game is to take part in lots of quizzes. By doing that you will not only hear what kind of questions are popular, you may also learn facts that will come in handy later. So you have to put in the hours – a lot of hours. I would say being a good quizzer is at least 50 per cent a matter of experience, so go out there and quiz.

A good quiz is priceless, a bad one is worthless. In a bad quiz, the questions are poorly researched or badly written, or the answers are so complex that only academics or experts in the field will know them. Ask yourself afterwards – will this quiz help you become a better player next time? If the answer is no, then don't go to that one again. If you are intent on becoming a superstar quizzer like myself, a word of warning: your research and your attendance at competitions will take up most of your time, so I would say it's better not to be in a relationship unless, like Paul and his husband Oliver, you plan to spend 10–12 hours a day quizzing together.

KNOW YOUR QUIZMASTER

If you go to a local quiz on a regular basis and you want to build up a reputation and improve your score, get to know your quizmaster. Find out what he or she is into, because their quiz will reflect their interests. That's the secret. Know what you're getting into. Go a couple of times, get a sense of the general feeling, and you'll know what kind of questions they are going to be asking next time.

Most regular quizmasters are creatures of habit. They tend to ask the same kind of questions week in, week out. I often claim that I can make a pretty good guess on the demographics of the setter just from seeing their questions. If the quiz is full of memes and Netflix/HBO/Amazon Prime TV shows from the last few years, the chances are your setter is in their twenties or early thirties and their questions will reflect that. Conversely, a veteran quizmaster will be asking you about the glorious music of the 60s, 70s and 80s and look surprised when a team of students doesn't know any of the songs.

One simple life hack is the current affairs round. Quizmasters often take these rounds from just one source, be it a newspaper or website. One time my colleague CJ de Mooi of *Eggheads* fame realized that a certain quizmaster in Caerphilly always took his questions from the BBC News website at some point in the early evening before the quiz. CJ is a first-class research quizzer and from then on it was maximum points every week.

The first time I took part in the British Championships, I got 44 and came 15th while others scored in the 70s. I was like, 'Wow, how the hell did that happen?' And my mate Richie said to me: 'Did you notice that you can find the answers to most of the questions in a book called *Brewer's Dictionary of Phrase and Fable*?' But there are other books out there that many serious quizzers use as a reference.

A guy called Trevor Montague has produced a book called *The A–Z of Almost Everything* which is a hardcore textbook of about 1,400 pages, stuffed full of all the things he thinks you need to know. It's a brilliant book, with everything in it that can help you do pretty well in a quiz. But bear in mind, this is his interpretation of what he thinks quizmasters may include in their quiz.

Ultimately you have to ask yourself, are you enjoying this quiz? If the answer is no, then it's time to stop going. The important thing is you've got to enjoy it. Just because a quiz might be suited to you, that doesn't make it enjoyable – it might be too easy, so you're not getting any satisfaction or gaining anything from it. My colleague Paul Sinha came up with a lovely paradox: 'The worse I do at a quiz, the better it is for me.' His argument is that if he got 99 out of 100 in a quiz, what was the point of him going? He just knew the answers and wasn't learning anything. Whereas if he only got 20 out of 100, he took on board the answers he didn't know because he appreciated it would stand him in good stead for future quizzes.

WHAT TYPE OF QUIZZER DO YOU WANT TO BE?

I enjoy being a quizzer. It's not really about winning prizes, it's about doing as well as I can in a competition, with an eye to a win. Most little league quizzes don't offer big prizes. Sometimes I've won enough money to buy a round of drinks, other times I've won a cake. Of course, as you grow as a quizzer and you gain more confidence and your reputation builds, you can start thinking about moving on to TV quiz shows where fortunes can indeed be won. When I appeared on shows like *Who Wants to Be a Millionaire?* I made more money in one sitting than I was earning in a year as a teacher! There is big money to be won, so quizzing can eventually become life changing. And who knows, if you've built up a solid quizzing reputation you may catch the eye of a TV producer who thinks you're just the person they're looking for.

THE CASUAL QUIZZER

My first question is the most obvious one: how seriously do you want to take this hobby? If you want to take part in the occasional quiz and just gofor the enjoyment of it, then more power to your elbow. Quizzes are entertainment first and foremost. Ninety-nine per cent of the quizzes held in the UK are for enjoyment, designed to raise money for charities or to get you spending money in the pub. If you have a good evening in fine company with excellent food and drink, then happy days. The good news is that there is every chance that there are several pub quizzes within a few miles of you, plus there always seem to be occasional quizzes held as fundraisers for good causes.

I am not a humble person. I freely admit that I am deeply flawed, but I do know a fair bit about the world of pub quizzes, and I have one aphorism I always share with quizmasters regardless of whether they ask for it: as a pub quiz host, you are there to sell beer. Most quizzes started as an attempt by the landlord or manager to improve takings on a quiet night. If you manage this, and some of the teams start coming in on non-quiz nights as well, then mine host will be very happy with you.

In my opinion a charismatic quiz host is better than a clever one. Ideally, though, you get one who is both. Their mission is to encourage people into the pub and entertain them so that they have a lovely time and spend a few pounds at the bar. Obviously it depends on the pub but a team that orders a meal before the quiz is the landlord's best friend, and by extension should be the quizmaster's, too. An unprofitable quiz is soon an ex-quiz.

A Machiavellian tactic to consider is working on the quizmaster, especially with a hint that you might not be returning. A smart quizmaster should at least think about what effect the loss of your team would have. Then you drop a hint as to what sort of stuff you would like to see in future quizzes. This might seem unethical, but serious quiz teams do this all the time – they work the quizmaster to influence the question balance on future quizzes. I am not sure if they are even doing it consciously, but I guarantee that a serious team will moan like crazy when there is a 'poor round', that is to say, a round that doesn't suit them.

THE SERIOUS PUB QUIZ TEAM

You play a few pub quizzes, occasionally you get the prize money. But the bug is starting to bite and you want to win more. So how do you go about it?

The first question to ask is, are you a specialist or all-rounder? The all-rounder obviously plays a bigger role in the team (with a much bigger earnings potential on TV). However, the sports/music/TV/film specialist is pretty much essential in a modern pub quiz team, especially given how diverse entertainment is these days.

Some lucky quizzers are fantastic at identifying people and objects on the picture rounds. Such people are priceless, especially as these rounds can produce some of the biggest points differentials. I work for Redtooth, which are probably the UK's biggest pub quiz company at the time of writing. They spend large amounts of money each year to license images from Getty Images and Reuters, to name but two major picture agencies. A similar thing occurs with the music rounds: prepared music quizzes such as Jukebox Junkie and Rock and Roll Bingo are copyright compliant. However, picture licensing fees are too expensive for many smaller companies and freelancers, so they lift images from newspapers and other publications instead, and the quality of the picture rounds can be highly variable, to put it mildly. Ah, the joys of trying to identify a poorly toned monochrome photocopy, which can be little more than various smudges of grey.

A quiz can be won or lost on the music round, and there are a lot of quizzers out there with a fantastic ear for a tune. There is a monthly quiz in Rhiwbina, a suburb of Cardiff, which several of the best teams in Wales attend for a chance to win a box of chocolates each. I think you can see my motivation immediately. One of our rival teams has an expert on pop music and they normally get at least 18 out of 20. If we don't lose more than a point or two, then we are in with a chance. In a situation like this, knowing your quizmaster becomes even more important. To put it bluntly, work on your weaknesses. If there are certain questions or topics that always come up on which you are losing ground to the top teams, can you close those gaps? If the host is always asking about current number ones, learn them. If he asks a question about Manchester United every other week, then make sure you read the sports pages.

So what kind of stuff should a serious team try to learn? I roughly break down knowledge into five levels and try to work from easier to harder. If it is something that a large chunk of the population knows, then so should you. My general maxim is don't give people easy wins over you. By that I mean know things like the capital of France or Germany – if they know the capital of Eritrea, then good on them.

As a personal aside, I leave a gap in my knowledge with soap operas. This is quite deliberate because, as I modestly say, Superman needs Kryptonite. If my job depended on it, however, I would be reading synopses of soap plot lines religiously and closing up that gap in my knowledge in a matter of weeks.

BECOMING A PRO QUIZZER
OR TV CELEBRITY

This is a bit like telling someone to spend at least a decade training for an Olympic sport whose rules might change or that might even be dropped from the line-up by the time the person is ready to compete. In my particular case, at the age of 43 a job opened up for which I was uniquely qualified. In hindsight, my career of teaching, quizzing and low-level sport left me with a set of skills that was perfect for this new job, but could I have foreseen it? No.

In the summer of 2009, I recorded five shows of *The Chase* and in 2010 I recorded fifteen more. The pay rate was comparable to a day's supply teaching. We held an end of series party at which we hoped for a renewal, but we were not holding our breath. Since then, of course, the show has gone from strength to strength, but the job requirements have also changed quite noticeably. Now future Chasers need to be both brilliant quizzers AND have a very strong personality. So many candidates have just one of the two, unfortunately.

However, if you examine the history of professional-based quiz shows in the UK and indeed the world, several of them have made it to 1,000 episodes, and just about all these shows share one wonderful quality that appeals to the modern TV scheduler: they are cheap to produce. Not just cheap but ridiculously cheap. Indeed, *Pointless*'s Richard Osman claimed in 2014 that an episode of *Pointless Celebrities* got similar ratings to *The X Factor* but was made on 1/24th of the budget.

So while it is not certain, I reckon there is every chance that there will be another pro-based quiz at some point in the next decade. Good luck!

SPECIALIST SUBJECTS
A–Z

THE 1960s

1. In April 1961, which Russian cosmonaut became the first person to fly in space?

2. The last 27 prisoners left which San Francisco prison, nicknamed 'the Rock', in March 1963?

3. The phrase 'This is not a pipe', written in French under a painting of a pipe, appears in a work by which Belgian surrealist artist who died in August 1967?

4. In 1966, which song, written by Lee Hazelwood, became an international number one hit single for Nancy Sinatra?

5. Which author, who died at the age of 46 in 1960, is perhaps best known for his works *The Fall*, *The Plague* and *The Outsider*?

6. In 1962, which American won his second Nobel Prize when he was awarded the Peace Prize for his fight against the nuclear arms race?

7. At which Welsh castle was Prince Charles formally acknowledged by the Queen as the Prince of Wales on 1 July 1969?

8. On 2 January 1967, which future American President was sworn in as the Governor of California?

9. What is the name of the breakaway state of the Congo whose leader, Moise Tshombe, announced its surrender in January 1963?

10. In 1965, Julie Andrews was awarded the Best Actress Oscar for her début role in which 1964 film?

11. What was the name of the coordinated series of attacks launched on Saigon and other major cities by the Viet Cong during the truce for New Year celebrations in January 1968?

12. In March 1969, who succeeded her friend Levi Eshkol to become the first female Prime Minister of Israel?

13. In February 1964, which supposed no-hoper defeated Sonny Liston to become World Heavyweight Boxing Champion for the first time?

14. Described as the 'greatest peacetime threat to Britain', what was the name of the oil tanker that ran aground on the Seven Stones Reef between Land's End and the Isles of Scilly in 1967?

15. In June 1962 which actress, along with her film producer husband Carlo Ponti, was tried for bigamy in Rome?

16. Whose last words, spoken to the Reverend Jesse Jackson in April 1968, are said to have been 'Be sure to sing "Precious Lord" tonight, and sing it well'?

17. Who became the first American to walk in space when he spent 14 minutes outside his Gemini 4 spacecraft in June 1965?

18. In 1964, the Great St Bernard road tunnel was opened though the Alps connecting Switzerland with which other country?

19. In the 1960 US Presidential election, which Republican candidate was beaten by John F Kennedy?

20. The song 'I'll Never Fall in Love Again', which was a hit for Dionne Warwick and topped the UK singles chart for Bobbie Gentry in 1969, was written by which composer and lyricist duo?

21. In March 1966, the first meeting in 400 years took place between the heads of the Roman Catholic and Anglican Churches. Michael Ramsay, the Archbishop of Canterbury, met which Pope? (Name and number needed.)

22. What is the name of the ravine in the Great Rift Valley in Tanzania in which anthropologist Louis Leakey found a series of human remains in February 1961?

23. In January 1962, which fashion designer and protégé of Christian Dior opened his own couture house in Paris?

24. Which non-fiction Truman Capote novel, first published in 1966, tells the story of the 1959 murders of four members of the Clutter family in Holcomb, Kansas?

25. 'The wind of change is blowing through this continent.' About which continent was Harold Macmillan speaking in a speech of 1960?

26. In July 1968, the courts decided that which novel by Hubert Selby Jr, set in New York, was not obscene?

27. In January 1965 British Prime Minister Winston Churchill died. He was buried at which stately home in Oxfordshire?

28. Which Asian city played host to the 1964 Summer Olympic games?

29. Which German-born American theoretical physicist became, in 1963, the second woman to win the Nobel Prize for Physics, for her work on the structure of the atomic nucleus?

30. About which pop group was record-shop owner Brian Epstein speaking in 1961 when he said: 'I want to manage those four boys. It wouldn't take me more than two and a half days a week'?

THE 1970s

1. Who became Britain's first female Prime Minister in 1979?

2. Many still dispute his death, but which popular musician died at his Graceland estate in 1977?

3. The Grant Hotel in San Diego hosted the first-ever comic-book convention. What are these events now more commonly known as?

4. Which toy answered children's questions with replies like 'It is certain' or 'Reply hazy, try again'?

5. The Watergate scandal led to the resignation of which US President?

6. 1974 welcomed the invention of which handy item of adhesive stationery?

7. Christine 'Chrissie' Watkins tragically lost her life in the opening scenes of which movie?

8. General Pinochet led a military coup in which country in 1973?

9. Who took over from Patrick Troughton as Doctor Who at the start of the decade?

10. The first what was transmitted in 1971?

11. The forerunner to today's Red Button, what service did the BBC launch in 1974?

12. The terrorist group Black September kidnapped and murdered 11 Israeli athletes from the Olympic Games held in which city?

13. The popular video game *Pong* made its debut in the 1970s. Which company released it?

14. What did a group of Chinese farmers discover in 1974?

15. Which character coined the phrase 'It's not easy being green'?

16. 'When you're weary, feeling small' are the opening lyrics of which Simon & Garfunkel song?

17. *Are You There God? It's Me, Margaret* is a book by which popular American young-adult fiction writer?

18. Wilnelia Merced, who later married Bruce Forsyth, won which contest in 1975?

19. Which song reached number one on 29 November 1975 and remained there until ABBA's 'Mamma Mia' knocked it off the top spot on 31 January 1976?

20. Princess Margaret announced her divorce from which commoner in 1978?

21. Which bike, launched in 1970, was branded as 'the hot one'?

22. On 1 July 1971, the 26th Amendment became law in the USA. What did it do?

23. What did *Tiswas* stand for?

24. Suriname was granted independence from which country in 1975?

25. What was the birth name of 1970s superstar Freddie Mercury?

26. What devastated the Australian city of Darwin on Christmas Eve in 1974?

27. In 1979, who was awarded the Nobel Peace Prize?

28. Which fictional creatures sold more records than any other UK act in 1974?

29. Bob Bryar, born as the decade closed on 31 December 1979, is the drummer with which American rock band?

30. In 1975 in Cambodia, Pol Pot led a revolution against the American-backed government of whom?

THE 1980s

1. In 1983, who became the first American woman in space, when she was part of the six-person crew of the *Challenger* space shuttle?

2. In January 1980, Queen Juliana announced that she would abdicate in favour of her daughter Beatrix in which European country?

3. In January 1986, the United States celebrated a national holiday for the first time that celebrates the birthday of which civil rights campaigner?

4. In March 1989, what was the name of the oil tanker that spilled around 240,000 barrels of oil after running aground on Prince William Sound in Alaska?

5. In July 1987, which 23-year-old became the first Briton to win the US Women's Open Golf Championship?

6. The US publisher De Witt Wallace, who died in March 1981, founded which magazine with his wife Lila Bell in 1922? The magazine was initially published only ten times a year.

7. Lindy and Michael Chamberlain were convicted of murder in Australia after claiming what type of wild dog had taken their baby, Azaria, in August 1982? The couple were pardoned in 1987.

8. What is the name of the ship owned by the environmental action group Greenpeace that was badly damaged by two explosions in Auckland harbour, New Zealand, in 1985?

9. In April 1984, which pop singer was shot dead after a violent argument with his father in Hancock Park, Los Angeles?

10. In February 1986, Jean-Claude Duvalier, the self-styled President for Life of Haiti, fled for France. What two-word name was he known by?

11. During the 1982 Paris–Dakar rally, Anne-Charlotte Verney and Jacky Garnier were lost in the Sahara desert for five days. They were the co-driver and mechanic of which driver?

12. In June 1989, a crowd of over 250,000 people gathered in Heroes' Square in Budapest for the reburial of which former Hungarian Prime Minister, who was executed in 1958?

13. Which item, considered one of the most sacred relics of the Roman Catholic Church, was declared a mediaeval fake by Oxford University and other institutions in 1988?

14. According to Andy Warhol, who died aged 58 in 1987, everyone will be famous for how many minutes?

15. Nicknamed the Butcher of Lyon, Nazi SS head Klaus Barbie was arrested in which South American country in 1983, where he had lived for many years under the name Altmann?

16. In a classic 1980 episode of the television soap opera *Dallas*, J R Ewing was shot by Kristen Shepard. Who was the father of the actress who played Kristen Shepard?

17. What was the name of the US warship that shot down an Iranian Airbus over the Persian Gulf in July 1988, killing all 286 people on board?

18. In April 1985, which media mogul bought 50 per cent of the 20th Century Fox film corporation at a cost of over £200 million?

19. What was the best-known nickname of jazz band leader William Basie, whose signature tune was 'One O'Clock Jump' and who died in 1984?

20. In 1989, which Asian country was readmitted to the Commonwealth after leaving in 1972?

21. In May 1980, which stratovolcano in Skamania County, Washington state, erupted?

22. In March 1985, who became the head of the Soviet Communist Party following the death of Konstantin Chernenko?

23. Which Colombian author was awarded the 1982 Nobel Prize for Literature? He was described as the greatest Colombian who ever lived by President Juan Manuel Santos.

24. Mike Tyson became the youngest World Heavyweight Boxing Champion when he knocked out which Jamaican-born fighter in November 1986?

25. Which religious building in Amritsar, occupied by Sikh militants, was stormed by Indian troops after a four-day siege in June 1984?

26. In 1981, which Motown legend had an international chart-topping single with the record 'Being With You'?

27. Which Asian capital city played host to the 1988 Summer Olympic Games?

28. Which film won eight awards at the 1983 Oscar ceremony, including wins for Richard Attenborough and Ben Kingsley?

29. In 1987 Fawn Hall described her employer as 'every secretary's dream of a boss'. To which assistant to Rear Admiral John Poindexter was Fawn Hall referring?

30. At which building in London did Prince Charles marry Lady Diana Spencer on 29 July 1981?

THE 1990s

1. In 1994, the USA gave approval for the growing of GM foods. What does GM stand for?

2. Larry Fortensky became whose final husband in her eighth and final wedding in 1991?

3. In 1994, Sony launched the first version of which iconic video game console?

4. Which group won the Eurovision Song Contest in 1997, the last win for Great Britain?

5. In 1990, the city of San Luis Obispo in California became the first city in the USA to ban what activity in bars and restaurants?

6. Also the name of a fictional island, which American space shuttle took off in March 1992 to study global warming?

7. What name, derived from the Japanese for 'lovable egg' or 'watch egg', was given to the virtual pet created by Aki Maita in 1996?

8. Which British scientist launched the website info.cern.ch in 1991?

9. In 1993, which country was partitioned in an action known as The Velvet Divorce?

10. In 1994, which country became the first African nation to have a population of over 100 million people?

11. In 1997 the Sky Tower, the tallest free-standing structure in the southern hemisphere, was opened in which New Zealand city?

12. In 1996, which businessman purchased the Miss Universe Organization?

13. Which *Neighbours* actor had their only UK single in 1990 with the number 16 hit 'Don't It Make You Feel Good'?

14. What is the name of the IBM-built supercomputer that became the first machine to win a game of chess against a World Champion, beating Garry Kasparov in 1996?

15. Unveiled in Japan in 1997, the first hybrid vehicle to go into full production, the Prius, is made by which company?

16. What was the name of the treaty signed on 7 February 1992 that founded the European Union?

17. Tommy Lee married and starred in an infamous honeymoon sex tape with Pamela Anderson in 1995. He was the drummer in which rock band?

18. Which fast-food restaurant opened its first UK outlet in 1996? It has the most fast-food outlets worldwide.

19. Actor Oliver Reed died in 1999 on the island of Malta. He was on the island filming which Oscar-winning movie?

20. Which 1993 Tim Burton animated film features a character called Jack Skellington?

21. Introduced in 1993, by what name is the North American Free Trade Agreement more commonly known?

22. In May 1992 plans were unveiled for a fifth terminal at which UK airport?

23. In 1995, Frenchwoman Jeanne Calment became the first-ever person to be confirmed to have lived to the age of 120. In interviews, she talked about meeting which artist when she was 13 years old?

24. 1999 saw combined NATO forces attack a sovereign state for the first time. Which country did they attack?

25. Which American airline, which featured a blue globe as its logo, ceased trading in 1991?

26. In July 1992, Abkhazia declared its independence from which former Soviet republic?

27. In 1995, which person, then aged 95, became the oldest person in the UK to receive hip-replacement surgery?

28. In 1999, which car company bought Rolls-Royce for $570 million?

29. In 1993, the terrorist group the Tamil Tigers assassinated the President of which country?

30. Up until 17 May 1990, when it was removed from the list, the World Health Organization shockingly included what on its list of diseases?

THE 2000s

1. In 2000, which country followed China to become the second country in the world to have a population of over one billion?

2. What was launched by a man called Jimmy Wales in January 2001? It now covers more than 6.5 million pages of the Internet.

3. Which US city hosted the 2002 Winter Olympics?

4. Which shopping centre in Birmingham opened in September 2003?

5. Launched in 2005, the Superjumbo passenger jet created by Airbus was given which designation?

6. Where did a crew dock for the first time on 2 November 2000?

7. Best known for playing Eleven in *Stranger Things*, which British actress was born in February 2004?

8. The first-ever YouTube video, uploaded in 2005, was filmed at what kind of location?

9. Having now sold over 2.2 billion units worldwide, the first generation of which device was launched by Steve Jobs in 2007?

10. Who was captured by the US Army in the town of Ad-Dawr, in December 2003?

11. James, the son of Prince Edward and Sophie Wessex, was born in 2007. He is also known by what title?

12. Which two island nations adopted the Euro as their currency in 2008?

13. Which Northern Irish prison closed in 2000 as a result of the Good Friday Agreement?

14. Which fiery Yorkshire cricketer died in July 2006?

15. Spotify was launched in October 2007. It is based in which country?

16. Which world-famous singer, born in 2001, has Pirate as one of her middle names?

17. What was the name of the army major who famously cheated in a 2001 episode of *Who Wants To Be A Millionaire?*

18. Who won his seventh and final Formula One title while driving for Ferrari in 2004?

19. Whose grave bears the epitaph 'I Told You I Was Ill'? He died in 2002.

20. Which former Prime Minister of Pakistan was assassinated at a protest rally in 2007?

21. Which famously neutral state finally joined the United Nations in September 2002?

22. The last signal from which NASA spacecraft was received in January 2003? It was over 12.3 billion km (7.6 billion miles) from Earth at the time.

23. Mark Zuckerberg launched Facebook in 2004, while he was a student at which university?

24. In 2008, who did Manchester United play against in the first-ever all-English Champions League Final?

25. What was the nickname of the stadium used as the central venue for the 2008 Olympics?

26. How old was Temba Tsheri when he climbed Mount Everest in 2001, becoming the youngest person to do so at that time?

27. Which two countries jointly hosted the 2002 Football World Cup?

28. Which sandbox video game was trialled by Mojang Studios in May 2009, prior to a worldwide release in 2011?

29. In 2007 Mauritania became the last country to outlaw what practice, finally making it illegal worldwide?

30. Which department of the US government was founded in October 2001, in response to the 9/11 terror attacks?

ANIMALS

1. Which is the world's largest species of lizard?

2. What is the two-word name of the seabird species that has the largest wingspan of any living bird?

3. The long, spiral tusk of which Arctic whale was often passed off as a unicorn horn during the Middle Ages?

4. The shoots and leaves of which fast-growing type of grass make up almost the entire diet of the giant panda?

5. Becoming extinct in 1870, the quagga was a subspecies of which African mammal?

6. What name is given to both the white whale and a species of sturgeon known for its caviar?

7. Which birds belong to the family Apodidae, which means 'without feet', in reference to the fact that the birds hardly ever land?

8. Karl von Frisch won a Nobel Prize in 1973 for decoding the meaning of the waggle dance performed by which creatures?

9. What name is given to the branch of zoology devoted to the study of fish?

10. What name is given to the vestigial nail, positioned similarly to a human thumb, found on the inner part of the paws of dogs and cats?

11. Which British duck species shares its name with a James Bond film starring Pierce Brosnan?

12. Meaning 'phantom insect', Phasmatodea is the scientific name for which order of very well-camouflaged creatures?

13. Before becoming extinct in the 17th century, the dodo had been endemic to which island?

14. Which large African bird of prey is so named because its crest of long feathers makes it look like it is carrying quill pens behind its ears?

15. Named after the Persian words for 'fire' and 'within', which group of amphibians are the only vertebrates than can regenerate lost legs?

16. Slugs and snails form which class of creatures, with a name deriving from the Greek for 'stomach-foot', within the Mollusca phylum?

17. Historically known as whalebone, what is the more common name for the filter-feeding system of krill-eating whales that is made up of a series of hair-like plates?

18. Which unit of weight is also an alternative name for the snow leopard?

19. What appropriate biblical name is given to the world's largest species of frog?

20. Which animal would you expect to find between a plastron and a carapace?

21. Including more than half of all bird species, what name is given to birds that are distinguished by having feet that are adapted for perching, including all songbirds?

22. To which phylum do mammals, birds, reptiles and amphibians all belong?

23. From the Greek word for 'gold', what name is given to the pupal form of a butterfly?

24. Which bird lays the largest eggs relative to its body size?

25. Found in birds, reptiles and some fish and insects, what name is given to the specialized stomach with a thick, muscular wall used for grinding up food?

26. The world's largest nocturnal primate, which species of lemur is noted for its extraordinarily long middle finger that it uses to extract grubs from inside tree trunks?

27. The first animals ever sent into space were which insects of the genus *Drosophila*, which are commonly used in genetic research?

28. Giving palaeontologists valuable evidence of the diets of dinosaurs and other prehistoric creatures, what name is given to fossilized faeces?

29. Which mammal has the scientific name *Phascolarctos cinereus*, meaning 'ash-coloured pouch bear'?

30. Which monkey takes its name from the fact that its dark brown cap is similar in colour to the hoods worn by its namesake monks?

ANSWER SMASH!

> *In this quiz, two facts are smashed together to give one three-word answer. For example: Legendary Northern Irish footballer who assists the groom? George Best man. (As always, give the FULL name.)*

1. Catherine Zeta-Jones's husband who wrote *The Hitchhiker's Guide to the Galaxy*?

2. Batman's alter ego was the ice hockey 'Great One'?

3. Drowned wife of Robert Wagner, with the Latin name *Columba palumbus*?

4. Blind singer who wrote *Great Expectations*?

5. Book about rabbits was a hit for Curiosity Killed The Cat?

6. Horror writer from Maine is a giant ape?

7. John Thaw character sends this dotty message?

8. 'Boom boom' puppet starred in a sitcom about a decorator?

9. Pirate emblem for secret agent actor?

10. Member of Take That who is obsessed with building a wall?

11. Tracking down *Jackal* actor with hounds?

12. Steve Coogan's creation sang with David Cassidy's kin?

13. Chelsea defensive legend who did a floral dance?

14. President of Nigeria (2010–2015) who solved puzzles from his windmill?

15. British political leader who was canonized in September 2016?

16. Record-breaking host visits the location for *Brideshead Revisited?*

17. Bookmaker situated in the closest town to Ben Nevis?

18. Magical entry to a thoroughfare of Muppetry?

19. Song and dance troupe whose members may have featured Betty Boothroyd and Cheryl Cole?

20. Sandy North African winner of the 1989 Cheltenham Gold Cup?

21. Peggy Mitchell actress lived at this Berkshire residence?

22. On-loan Chelsea/Swansea striker, assassinated in 1865?

23. Jennifer Saunders's comedy partner has some chips?

24. Heavyweight boxer who judges on *Strictly* (You know what I mean, 'Arry)?

25. As played by Richard Gibson, this *'Allo 'Allo* Nazi carries a sharp weapon.

26. Inquisitive punctuation who won seven swimming Golds at the 1972 Munich Olympics?

27. *Rising Damp*'s Miss Jones wins a prestigious cycle race in Paris? (More than three words required.)

28. Calm down, dear – this *Death Wish* director is singing a 1980 Abba number one? (More than three words required.)

29. 1963 Crystals hit about an anchorman?

30. Snooker maximum and good luck in the theatre?

> *After taking the quiz, Mark said: 'With this one, I couldn't just "bang out the answers" but when I slipped up, I understood how the answer works. Great quiz.'*

ART

Before he took the quiz, Mark said: 'I know "quiz" art, that is to say the kind of questions about art you get in a quiz. But I don't go to art galleries and I'm renowned for not being the best in this category.'

1. One of Andy Warhol's best-known works depicts 50 images of which actress appearing in the 1953 film *Niagara*?

2. Thought to be a portrait of the Italian noblewoman Lisa Gherardini, *La Gioconda* is an alternative name for which very famous painting?

3. Henri de Toulouse-Lautrec is probably best remembered for his paintings depicting which famous cabaret club near Montmartre?

4. What type of objects are depicted melting in Salvador Dali's painting *The Persistence of Memory*?

5. In Botticelli's painting *The Birth of Venus*, on what type of object is the title goddess standing?

6. *Arrangement in Grey and Black No. 1* is the official title of which very famous 1871 painting?

7. What name do we give to a work of art that is divided into three sections, often three carved panels that are hinged together?

8. What name is given to the method of post-Impressionist painting, most famously employed by Georges Seurat, in which tiny dots of colour are used to create an image?

9. During the 1890s, which French artist completed a series of famous paintings of Rouen Cathedral?

10. Francis Bacon famously produced a 1953 reworking of which Spanish painter's 1650 portrait of Pope Innocent X?

11. Which Grant Wood painting of 1930 depicts a farmer standing in front of his house with his spinster daughter?

12. In Delacroix's *Liberty Leading the People*, the title character holds a musket in her left hand, but what does she hold in her right?

13. In which mural-painting technique particularly associated with the Italian Renaissance is paint applied directly to wet plaster on a wall or ceiling?

14. Robert Mapplethorpe, Robert Capa, Robert Frank and Robert Doisneau were all famous names in which field of the arts?

15. The painter Doménikos Theotokópoulos was born on Crete in 1541 but became famous after moving to Toledo. By what name is he now better known?

16. The Ashcan School movement of the late 19th and early 20th centuries sought to depict everyday life in which major city?

17. The Australian artist Sydney Nolan is best known for a series of paintings of which famous bushranger and outlaw who was hanged in 1880?

18. Which fruit covers the face of René Magritte in his famous 1964 self-portrait *The Son of Man*?

19. What colour is the dress worn by the bride in Van Eyck's famous *Arnolfini Portrait*?

20. Marie Grosholtz's first sculpture was of the French novelist Voltaire. Born in Strasbourg in 1761, she is better known by what name today?

21. Which term means 'light-dark' in Italian and is used to describe the use of strongly contrasting light and shade in a work of art?

22. Which mammals are a recurring motif in much of the work of Frida Kahlo? She kept several of these animals at her home and typically incorporated them in her self-portraits.

23. *The Three Graces* is among the best-known works of which neoclassical Italian sculptor?

24. Which French term, meaning 'trick of the eye', is given to a style of painting that emphasizes the illusion of tactile and spatial qualities, often giving the effect of photographic realism?

25. A photograph entitled *Clearing Winter Storm* is one of the best-known works of which American photographer, known for his shots of Yosemite National Park and the wider American West?

26. Which artistic group was founded in 1911 by Wassily Kandinsky and Franz Marc, among others, in response to the rejection of Kandinsky's painting *Last Judgement* from an exhibition?

27. Thomas Cole and Frederic Church were leading members of an American school of painting named after which river?

28. Born in 1841, which artist, known for her works *The Cradle* and *Lady at her Toilette*, was the only woman to display paintings at the first Impressionist exhibition in 1874?

29. Michelangelo famously created a marble statue of David. But the most famous work of which Renaissance artist is probably his bronze statue of David?

30. The French post-Impressionist painter Henri Rousseau is perhaps best known for *The Sleeping Gypsy*. What type of animal is sniffing the title character in that painting?

BIOLOGY

1. What gaseous substance, which comprises around 0.04 per cent of the air, is fixed into sugars and starches by plants during photosynthesis?

2. Named after a hero of the Trojan War, what name is given to the tendon that connects the calf muscles to the heel bone?

3. What powdery substance released by plants and carried by insects or wind contains male sperm cells and causes allergies such as hay fever?

4. Sharing its name with a co-operative board game released in 2008 by Z-Man Games, what term describes the outbreak of an infectious disease across several countries or continents?

5. Short-interfering, transfer, ribosomal and messenger are types of what cellular macromolecule that mediates and regulate gene expression within a cell?

6. What seven-letter anatomical name is given to the flat bone that constitutes the kneecap?

7. *Variola major* and *Variola minor* cause which infectious disease, which is said to have been eradicated in the wild in 1977?

8. Deficiency of what vitamin, sometimes known as ascorbic acid, results in the disease scurvy?

9. What letter of the alphabet is shared by a vitamin complex that contains thiamine and niacin, and a type of cell in the immune system that produces antibodies?

10. What geological period, the name of which means 'coal-bearing', followed the end of the Devonian period 358.9 million years ago? It is the period in which amphibians became dominant.

11. What name is given to the protective liquid surrounding a developing foetus in the womb? This fluid has historically been sampled in order to obtain genetic information about the foetus.

12. What five-letter word is shared by gaseous exchange pores in the surface of a leaf and an artificial orifice made in the abdomen when sections of diseased intestine are removed?

13. An anti-hypertensive drug is used in order to reduce the reading of what vital sign?

14. What sexually transmitted disease caused by the spirochaete bacterium *Treponema pallidum* is characterized by skin rashes and sores around the genitals in its early stages? Many years after initial infection, it can cause blindness, dementia and damage to the nerves in the limbs in its later stages.

15. Which drug used in the induction and maintenance of anaesthesia and in the treatment of severe depression is also a street drug with the nicknames Kit Kat, Cat Valium and Special K?

16. Ommatidia are compound forms of which sense organ in insects?

17. In which part of the human body would one find the metatarsal bones?

18. Derived from a Greek name for the study of 'houses', what term is given to the branch of biology that studies the relationships between organisms and their habitat?

19. What name is given to the 'rest and digest' part of the autonomic (involuntary) nervous system?

20. American Beauty, Dorothy Perkins, Iceberg, Golden Showers and Peace are famous varieties of what summer-flowering plant?

21. With a six-letter name beginning with C, what polymer of N-acetylglucosamine is a primary component of fungal cell walls and the exoskeletons of some insects?

22. What is the name of the gas with the formula C_2H_4, which acts as a hormone in plants to cause ripening and flowering?

23. What flavivirus, which could cause birth defects and be transmitted with no symptoms, caused a pandemic in 2015 and 2016 as it spread eastwards across the Pacific? It takes its name from a Ugandan forest.

24. Which neurotransmitter has receptors that are both nicotinic and muscarinic?

25. Named for a Canadian physician, what eponymous term is given to a condensed, inactivated X chromosome viewed under a microscope? This physician shares a name with an Irish virologist who gave her name to a virus causing infectious mononucleosis.

26. With an onomatopoeic name that comes from the repetitive whistling noise made when the animals feel threatened, what name is given to any of four species from the tiny antelope genus *Madoqua* found in the eastern and southern African bushlands? Günther's, Kirk's, Salt's and Silver are the four species, which stand at 30–40cm (12–16in) to the shoulder.

27. Sometimes known as cranesbill, what genus of flowering plants shares its name with a Michelin-star-winning restaurant run by Rasmus Kofoed in Copenhagen?

28. Which cytogeneticist won the Nobel Prize in Physiology or Medicine in 1983 for her discovery of transposable genetic elements in maize plants?

29. With a name that means 'whip' in Latin, what term is given to the tail-like appendage of mammalian and plant sperm cells, and to bacterial appendages that drive motility?

30. What neurodegenerative disease caused by a CAG repeat expansion in the HTT gene on Human Chromosome 4 is characterized by flitting, jerky movements known as chorea, dementia and severe mental health problems, such as depression and psychosis? The musician Woody Guthrie died of complications of this condition in 1967.

CHEMISTRY

Before doing this quiz, Mark said: 'Ah, this is a really strong category for me. I predict 28 out of 30!' Spoiler alert: that didn't happen. This is a particularly tough set of questions, so be warned.

1. Graphite in pencils is an allotrope of which element with atomic number 6?

2. The ignition of what light, flammable gas caused the *Hindenburg* air disaster in 1937?

3. Francis Crick, James Watson and Maurice Wilkins won the 1962 Nobel Prize in Physiology or Medicine for the discovery of which fundamental biological molecule?

4. With the formula H_2SO_4, what acid did serial killer John George Haigh use to dispose of the bodies of his victims?

5. In 2017, a feed called Bovaer was given to cattle in Alberta, Canada, with the aim of reducing their production of what greenhouse gas with the formula CH_4?

6. Although it can contain 0.5 per cent silver, galena is a sulphide ore and the main one of which toxic heavy metal? Paolo Nutini had a pencil full of this in a 2009 single from the album *Sunny Side Up*.

7. With a name derived from the Greek term for 'idle', which noble gas is the most abundant in the earth's atmosphere at 0.9 per cent?

8. When proteins are digested in the stomach and small intestine by enzymes, they are broken down into small peptides and their constituent units with what two-word name? Examples of these substances are glycine, glutamate and tyrosine.

9. Mentioned in Radiohead's song 'No Surprises' in an unusual 'handshake', which highly toxic gas can arise from faulty central heating systems? Tell-tale signs include soot around a boiler or a yellow flame instead of a blue flame.

10. As chemical inhibitors of the enzyme HMG-CoA reductase, drugs such as atorvastatin and simvastatin are given with the aim of reducing which 'bad' molecule in blood that forms part of a complex called LDLs (low-density lipoproteins)?

11. The leaves from the willow tree (genus *Salix*) are the source of the precursor of which very common analgesic and anti-platelet drug, frequently given after a stroke or heart attack?

12. Which metallic element is the crucial central component of the porphyrin ring in chlorophyll molecules? It is also used in flares, fireworks and sparklers.

13. Mentioned in the title of a Nirvana song, which alkali metal is used in the treatment of bipolar disorder and, occasionally, in refractory cluster headaches?

14. As strong as steel but weighing only half as much, which element used in prosthetic hips is also used in white paint, and is a component of Australian singer-songwriter Sia, according to a David Guetta single of 2011?

15. Also a term for the use of performance-enhancing drugs, what term is given to the introduction of impurities into a semiconductor to modify its conduction properties?

16. The play *Photograph 51* by Anna Ziegler focuses on which X-ray crystallographer whose photograph was key for deciphering the double helix structure of DNA? She died from ovarian cancer aged 37 in 1958.

17. With atomic number 46 and sharing its name with a London theatre, which chemical element found in car catalytic converters was discovered in 1803 by William Hyde Wollaston?

18. What term is given to the passage of petroleum vapour over a catalyst bed causing its break-up into lighter, more valuable hydrocarbon fractions? This term is often used by Gromit's master in Aardman Animation films.

19. Who was the tax official and eminent chemist who identified the role of oxygen in combustion? His death by guillotine on 8 May 1794 led Joseph-Louis Lagrange to comment, 'Only a moment to cut off that head and a hundred years may not give us another one like it.'

20. Aqua regia is a mix of three parts hydrochloric acid and one part of which strong acid that is also known as aqua fortis?

21. Which metal atom is at the centre of a vitamin B12 corrin ring?

22. With atomic number 76, what is the densest naturally occurring element, used for staining as a tetroxide in electron microscopy?

23. The former student of Marie Curie, French physicist Marguerite Perey discovered which chemical element in 1939, by purifying samples of lanthanum that contained actinium? Loss of an alpha particle turned actinium into this element.

24. A process that revolutionized palaeontology by assisting the accurate ageing of fossils was developed in 1949 by American physical chemist Willard Libby. What two-word term, not offered by Bumble or Tinder, is given to this method?

25. The production of messenger RNA involves the splicing out of which often large non-coding components from between the exons?

26. Venki Ramakrishnan, Tom Steitz and Ada Yonath won the 2009 Nobel Prize in Chemistry for their work on the structure and function of which cellular organelle where protein synthesis occurs?

27. Both DNA and RNA contain the bases adenine, guanine and cytosine, but what base is used in place of thymine in RNA?

28. What name is given to the repetitive protective DNA sequences located at the ends of chromosomes? Their shortening, which occurs when cells divide, may contribute to ageing.

29. Which Swedish physical chemist and 1903 Nobel Prize winner was the first to try to estimate the extent to which CO_2 warms the atmosphere? He gave his name to a famous 'rate' equation for the effect of temperature on the rate of chemical reactions.

30. Jennifer Doudna and Emmanuelle Charpentier won the 2020 Nobel Prize in Chemistry for their work on which gene-editing system with a six-letter name, an acronym for a set of bacterial DNA sequences that have revolutionized molecular medicine? Despite its name, you wouldn't use it for salad.

After doing the quiz, Mark said: 'Wow, that was tough. I reckon people will struggle to get into double figures with this one.'

COMPUTER GAMES

Before taking this quiz, Mark said: 'Hmm, this could go either way for me. It could be a score of 5 or 25!'

1. The Switch, Wii and GameCube are all consoles made by which company?

2. Dance trends such as The Floss originated from which video game? Players start on the Battle Bus before competing in a 100-player Battle Royale.

3. The Ghost Gang, which includes Blinky, Pinky, Inky and Clyde, is found in which classic arcade game?

4. Wayne Rooney, Lionel Messi and Kylian Mbappé have all been cover stars of which video game series? The 23rd edition was confirmed to be the final iteration under its current name.

5. Which game involves manoeuvring a growing line that becomes a primary obstacle to itself? A variant was included on Nokia phones, causing a boom in this game's popularity.

6. What is the name of the AI character who helps Master Chief in the *Halo* series? She shares her name with a virtual assistant.

7. Released in June 2022 on the Nintendo Switch, *Battle League* is the latest instalment of the *Strikers* series of which Nintendo character?

8. Which game by Psyonix, with a strong presence on the esports scene, can be described as 'soccer, but with super-powered cars'?

9. Now a Netflix series starring Henry Cavill, which award-winning video game series follows the lead character Geralt of Rivia?

10. In which free-to-play puzzle game, released by King, do players complete levels by swapping coloured pieces of sugary foods?

11. Which location completes the titles of these games by LucasArts? *The Secret of…, The Curse of…* and *Escape From…*

12. Ryu, Chun Li and Vega are all selectable characters in which game series?

13. Sharing its name with an energy drink, which company created *Red Dead Revolver* and *Red Dead Redemption 1* and *2*?

14. *Indiana Jones, Harry Potter* and the *Star Wars* series have all been part of which group of video games? In these games, points are scored by collecting 'studs' found on 'bricks'.

15. Which marsupial, an early mascot for PlayStation, has a sister called Coco and an archnemesis called Dr Neo Cortex?

16. In which series of life simulation games do the titular characters go about their day-to-day lives with a diamond-shaped 'plumbob' hovering above their heads?

17. Which video games series features Samus Aran, a bounty hunter clad in an armoured 'power suit'? The first 3D version of this game had the subtitle 'Prime'.

18. The three cities that make up the map in the original *Grand Theft Auto* series are Liberty City, Vice City and which other destination?

19. Available on most VR headsets, which Golden Joystick award-winning game takes place in a surrealistic neon environment, in which the player has to slice blocks representing musical beats?

20. In the most popular game mode of CS:GO, two teams attack and defend bomb sites. What does the CS stand for in the title of this first-person shooter game?

21. Lumbridge and Varrock are two cities in which MMORPG created by Jagex? This is the world's largest and most-updated free-to-play MMORPG.

22. In *Mario Kart*, what alliterative name is given to the power-up that turns the user into a projectile which fires along the track, knocking over anyone in its way?

23. What is the last trophy a player can win on every game on PlayStation?

24. Which platform battle royale game, in which up to 60 players compete in a series of mini games until only one is crowned the winner, became free to play in June 2022?

25. Which survival horror game takes place in a pizzeria filled with hostile animatronic characters? The player controls an employee who must survive the night in the building.

26. Which 2D hack-and-slash game by independent developer The Behemoth focuses on four colourful knights who are tasked with saving four princesses who have been abducted by a dark wizard?

27. Which cross-platform game by Blizzard is a turn-based card game in which players use mana to summon minions to defeat the opposition's hero?

28. Globox is the best friend of which character who has hands and feet but no arms and legs? Games in this series include *Hoodlum's Revenge* and *Raving Rabbids*.

29. What kind of 'hero' are you if you can match notes scrolling on the screen to coloured fret buttons on the controller, strumming in time to the music in order to score points?

30. Which famous streamer, who found fame by streaming *Fortnite* on Twitch, failed to get the citizens of New York to Floss in Times Square?

FASHION

1. With cinched waistlines and full skirts, which French fashion designer created the New Look following World War Two? Natalie Portman has been a face of an eponymous fragrance for this fashion house.

2. Which former French Grand Slam tennis star created a tennis shirt with a crocodile logo, reflecting his nickname?

3. The shapewear label SKIMS was created by which internet breaker, who controversially wore a dress previously famously worn by Marilyn Monroe to the 2022 Met Gala?

4. Naomi Campbell toppled off a pair of vertiginous purple platform heels at the 1993 catwalk show of which British punk-inspired fashion designer and former girlfriend of Malcolm McLaren?

5. Which former Spice Girl's fashion label debuted at New York Fashion Week in 2008?

6. 'Killer-heel' designer Manolo Blahnik launched a collaborative line of more practical footwear with which German orthopaedic footwear designer first established in 1774? Known for shoes with wide footbeds, the company's classic designs include the Madrid and Arizona sandals and the Boston clog.

7. Which German fashion designer for Fendi, Chloé and Chanel, who died in 2019, leaving a very rich cat called Choupette, famously opined that 'sweatpants are a sign of defeat'?

8. Featured in a 2018 documentary film, which British fashion designer who gained fame at Givenchy took his own life in 2010? His designs include the notorious buttock-skimming Bumster trousers, as featured in his first collection for his own label in 1993.

9. Founded in 1978 by Marco Boglione in Italy, which sportswear label named for a Greek letter features two women sitting back to back on its logo?

10. Which Swedish fashion conglomerate owns the concept brands COS, & Other Stories, ARKET and Cheap Monday?

11. Originally a producer of weatherproof survival suits for North Sea oilmen and shipworkers, which Norwegian outdoor clothing brand was appropriated by hip-hop artists such as LL Cool J and Funkmaster Flex in the 1990s?

12. Which American fashion designer launched his Polo menswear range with its iconic logo in 1968?

13. The famously revealing safety-pin dress worn by Elizabeth Hurley to the premiere of *Four Weddings and a Funeral* in 1994 was designed by which Italian fashion house, whose figurehead met an untimely end in 1997?

14. Which swimwear manufacturer known for notoriously tight 'budgie-smuggler' swim briefs was founded in 1914 in Bondi Beach, Australia, by Alexander MacRae?

15. Who is the Ghanaian editor-in-chief of British *Vogue* and the European editorial director of the Condé Nast group?

16. With a name that sounds like two lagers, which supermodel, It-girl and granddaughter of the 11th Duke of Devonshire died by suicide aged 50 in December 2020?

17. The first-ever solo male cover star of *Vogue* magazine in 2020, which former One Direction singer launched his own make-up range, called Pleasing?

18. Minimalist German fashion designer Jil Sander launched the +J line with which mass-market Japanese brand in 2009?

19. Which Spanish fashion label, notable for its Triple S and Speed trainers, was worn by The Simpsons in a short animated film specially made for Paris Fashion Week in October 2021?

20. Established as a company selling clothing for outdoor adventurers in 1892, which company rebranded itself as a purveyor of hipster casualwear in the 1990s and drew controversy for fat-shaming its staff and customers? The American pop group LFO liked girls who wore this label in their 1999 song 'Summer Girls'.

21. Which Venezuelan fashion designer and dresser of first ladies including Jackie Onassis, Laura Bush and Michelle Obama markets the fragrances Bad Boy and Good Girl?

22. Melania Trump caused controversy in 2018 by wearing a jacket featuring the words 'I Really Don't Care, Do U?' when visiting migrant children. From which Spanish high-street fashion chain was the jacket bought?

23. Which supermodel, Victoria's Secret Angel and host of the TV series *Project Runway* launched her own IT venture in 2019, encouraging girls to learn computer coding?

24. A face of Marks & Spencer menswear since 2013, which English fashion model was featured in a 2013 coffee-table book by the fashion house Dolce & Gabbana? He has also been a brand ambassador for Johnnie Walker Blue Label.

25. The Tony Award-nominated 2016 musical *Warpaint* depicts the rivalry between Elizabeth Arden and which Polish-American founder of an eponymous beauty empire in the 1900s?

26. Which eponymous Italian sportswear label, launched by a former Italian tennis champion in 1966, began sponsoring Novak Djokovic in 2009? Originally focused on tennis, in the 1980s the company expanded into leisurewear, including the 'Dallas' tracksuit.

27. Which Nottinghamshire hosiery brand founded in 1919 is named after an alliteratively named racehorse?

28. Known for her flamboyant style and round glasses, which 100-year-old fashion icon launched her sell-out collection in collaboration with H&M in April 2022?

29. Which upmarket British perfumer's fragrances include The Tragedy of Lord George, The Blazing Mr Sam and The Coveted Duchess Rose?

30. Who was the first make-up artist to be made a British Dame in 2021?

FILM

Before taking the quiz, Mark said: 'I'm pretty good at this category, as long as the questions are about mass-market films. I'm not so hot on arthouse cinema!'

1. What type of animal terrorizes the people of Amity Island in the film *Jaws*?

2. Who is the only actor to appear in all five films in the *Die Hard* film franchise?

3. *The Age of Ultron*, *Infinity War* and *End Game* are subtitles of films about which group of superheroes?

4. Which actor's two Best Actor Academy Awards came for the films *Philadelphia* and *Forrest Gump*?

5. Julie Andrews sings the song 'Supercalifragilistic-expialidocious' in which 1964 film?

6. Which is the only one of the dwarfs in the Disney film *Snow White and the Seven Dwarfs* who doesn't have a beard?

7. Which Oscar-winning song plays during the final scene of the film *Dirty Dancing*?

8. Which actress played Belle in the 2017 live-action remake of the Disney animated film *Beauty and the Beast*?

9. In the film *First Blood*, Sylvester Stallone's character John Rambo is a veteran of which war?

10. The band Berlin's single 'Take My Breath Away' and the Kenny Loggins song 'Danger Zone' feature on the soundtrack of which 1986 film?

11. When he was playing Shrek, the actor Mike Myers adopted what accent?

12. In the *Back to the Future* films, what speed must the DeLorean car achieve in order to travel through time?

13. Which actress played Adam Sandler's love interest in the films *The Wedding Singer*, *50 First Dates* and *Blended*?

14. In the film *Hidden Figures*, the characters played by Taraji P Henson, Octavia Spencer and Janelle Monaé all work in which field of the sciences?

15. Michelle Pfeiffer played which villain in the film *Batman Returns*? Anne Hathaway played the same character in *The Dark Knight Rises*.

16. Which sport is featured in the film *Cool Runnings*?

17. What kind of monster does Harry Potter encounter in the Chamber of Secrets in the film *Harry Potter and the Chamber of Secrets*?

18. In the film *The Last Jedi*, the 2m 10cm (6ft 11in) tall actor Joonas Suotamo took over the role of which *Star Wars* character from Peter Mayhew?

19. Which 2022 film based on a video game series sees Tom Holland play the treasure hunter Nathan Drake?

20. What religious artifact does Indiana Jones try to recover in the film *Indiana Jones and the Last Crusade*?

21. Future American President Ronald Reagan starred in the 1951 film *Bedtime for Bonzo*. What was Bonzo?

22. Which major real-life crime is central to the plot of the 1988 Phil Collins film *Buster*?

23. A plan to sink a German gunboat called the *Königin Luise*, which is patrolling a large lake, is central to which 1951 film? The film won Humphrey Bogart his only Oscar for Best Actor.

24. In *Rocky IV*, the boxing match at the end of the film between Rocky Balboa and Ivan Drago takes place in Moscow on what day of the year?

25. The 2019 film *Doctor Sleep* was the sequel to which 1980 psychological horror film?

26. In which film did Arnold Schwarzenegger first say his iconic line 'I'll be back'?

27. Which Bond villain who appeared in the films *The Spy Who Loved Me* and *Moonraker* only says four words across both films, with those words being, 'Well, here's to us'?

28. Which film that won seven Academy Awards involves its lead characters trying to con a gangster using a scheme known as 'the wire'?

29. More famous as a film director, who wrote the story that was the basis for the film *Natural Born Killers*?

30. What is the name of the school that the main characters in the first *American Pie* film attend?

FOOD AND DRINK

Before he took this quiz, Mark said: 'Oh no, this is traditionally my weakest subject. I don't cook!'

1. Which alcoholic spirit is made by fermenting then distilling sugarcane molasses or sugarcane juice?

2. A pizza topped with ham and pineapple is named after which US state?

3. In which US state is Jack Daniel's whiskey made?

4. Which chocolate brand produces Bournville chocolate, Dairy Milk, Caramel and Creme Eggs?

5. Which cocktail consisting of vodka, triple sec, cranberry juice and lime juice shares its name with a fashion magazine?

6. What is the most expensive spice in the world?

7. George Clooney, Mike Meldman and Rande Gerber founded Casamigos, a brand of what type of alcohol?

8. Which fruit is used in a tarte citron?

9. Which TV chef released the book *How to Be a Domestic Goddess* in 2000?

10. Which meat is traditionally served with mint sauce?

11. If an Indian dish is described as saag, what does it contain?

12. In the film *The Big Lebowski*, what is The Dude's drink of choice?

13. Which spice provides the main flavouring and colour of goulash?

14. Calamari is the Italian word for which cephalopod?

15. Wagyu beef is native to which Asian country?

16. The Fat Duck restaurant is run by which celebrity chef, known for his experimental cooking?

17. Which dessert was launched by Wall's in 1982? It is best known for its vanilla and mint flavours.

18. Which Italian restaurant chain, known for its doughballs, was founded by Peter Boizot in 1965?

19. A festival in which participants throw tomatoes is held in which European country?

20. Which French vodka brand is named after a species of waterfowl?

21. Which American fast-food chain, which made a return to the UK in 2022, is known for its Baconator burger and fries?

22. Ackee and saltfish is the national dish of what Caribbean island?

23. What is the name of the West African rice dish made with tomatoes, onions, vegetables, meat and spices?

24. Ray Kroc bought which fast-food restaurant in 1955? This chain moved its headquarters to downtown Chicago in 2018.

25. Which soft drink was created by Charles Alderton in Texas and launched in 1885? It preceded Coca-Cola by one year.

26. What chain of steakhouses and cocktail bars was founded by Will Beckett and Huw Gott in 2006? Primarily based in London, it also has restaurants in Edinburgh, Manchester and New York City.

27. Which type of tea is grown and processed in its namesake region in West Bengal? A Wes Anderson film is set in this region.

28. Which chef wrote the book *Kitchen Confidential*?

29. Once the largest owner of alcoholic brands in the world, which now defunct Canadian company lends it name to a skyscraper on Park Avenue?

30. A Moscow Mule is often served in a cup made of what type of metal?

GEOGRAPHY

Before taking the quiz, Mark said: 'I'm pretty confident on Geography, I reckon I should get into the low 20s at least.'

1. Which country has the world's longest coastline, measuring 243,042km (151,000 miles)?

2. Etna and Stromboli are examples of what geographical feature?

3. What is the capital of Mexico?

4. What is the world's largest ocean by area?

5. What country ends with the letter Q?

6. What country formerly ruled Iceland?

7. Franz Josef is a 12km- (7½ mile-) long what in New Zealand's South Island?

8. What river flows through the Grand Canyon?

9. What do the flags of Albania, Sri Lanka and Kazakhstan all contain?

10. What is the most-used scale to measure earthquakes?

11. How many stars are there on the Australian flag?

12. Rocks that form due to the cooling of molten lava are called what?

13. How many time zones does Russia have?

14. What cape sits at the southern tip of Africa?

15. Which famous broadcaster and biologist was born on 8 May 1926?

16. Does Japan's traffic run on the left or right?

17. Formed when a wide meander of a river is cut off, creating a free-standing body of water. What am I?

18. What state is Mount Rushmore located in?

19. What is the national dish of Hungary?

20. Designed to alleviate the housing shortages following World War Two, which Hertfordshire town became the UK's first new town in 1946?

21. Iqaluit, which means 'place of fish', is the biggest community on the largest island in the Arctic Archipelago. Name this island.

22. Which US city is located on Puget Sound?

23. In 1997 which country punched out their ousted leader's face on banknotes until they had time to print new ones?

24. The Atlas mountain range spans which three countries?

25. On which major African river will you find the Victoria Falls?

26. Which country is home to the fewest people per square mile?

27. What city lies on the western shore of the Caspian Sea?

28. By definition, a megacity is an urban area with what population?

29. In Venezuela, what name is given to almost constant lighting strikes, averaging over 100 strikes per hour?

30. What is the science of clouds called?

HISTORY PRE-1900

1. King Richard I of England was known by what nickname due to his great courage and prowess in battle?

2. Captain William Kidd, Calico Jack Rackham, Anne Bonny, Captain Henry Morgan and Edward Teach, better known as Blackbeard, are all famous for having what occupation?

3. In which American town did a series of Witch Trials take place in 1692, which resulted in the execution of 20 people accused of witchcraft?

4. What disease, which spread throughout Asia and Europe between 1346 and 1353 and is thought to have been spread by fleas that lived on rats, is estimated to have killed as much as a third of the world's population?

5. Abraham Lincoln was the first President of the USA who represented which political party?

6. Joan of Arc came to prominence during which war fought between England and France which, despite its name, lasted 116 years?

7. Julius Caesar was assassinated on 15 March 44 BC during a meeting of the Roman Senate. What name was this date given in Ancient Rome?

8. Which King of France was executed in 1793 during the French Revolution?

9. When Queen Isabella of Castille married King Ferdinand of Aragon in 1469, the kingdoms would eventually merge to form which modern-day country?

10. In the War of the Roses, what colour rose represented the forces of the House of York?

11. At the age of only 26, Edward Rutledge was the youngest person to sign what document?

12. The real-life Macbeth reigned as King of the Scots from 1040 to 1057. Who was the King of England at the time of his death?

13. Who, from a hidden vantage point, was allegedly the only person to see Lady Godiva, the wife of Leofric, the Earl of Mercia, as she rode a horse naked through the streets of Coventry? He gives his name to people today who do similar actions.

14. Bucephalus, who died in 326 BC at the age of 29, played a key role in the conquests of Alexander the Great. What was Bucephalus?

15. Other than his final wife, Catherine Parr, who was the only one of Henry VIII's six wives to outlive him?

16. Sharing its name with an unfashionable haircut and a type of fish, what is a five-pointed star known as in heraldry?

17. Which Greek philosopher was the teacher of his fellow Greek philosopher Plato?

18. What name was given to the infamous British serial killer who was never caught, despite killing at least five woman in the Whitechapel area of London in 1888?

19. Now perhaps more famous for playing an important role in an acclaimed musical, who was the first person to hold the position of Vice-President of the USA who didn't subsequently go on to become president?

20. Which Ancient Roman road connected Rome and the city of Brindisi?

21. The Dragon Throne was the name given to the throne of the ruler of which empire?

22. In AD 312, the Roman Emperor Constantine disbanded which organization that had acted as the emperor's bodyguard up to that time?

23. Meaning drifter or wanderer, what name was given to a samurai warrior who didn't have a lord or master?

24. Thought to have been destroyed by an earthquake in the 15th century, which was the last of the Seven Wonders of the Ancient World to be destroyed?

25. Considered to be Europe's oldest city and found on the island of Crete, what was the name of the city at the centre of the Minoan civilization?

26. With bases in Lübeck, Hamburg and numerous other European cities, what was the name of the association of merchant guilds that dominated Northern European trade between the 15th and 18th centuries?

27. Which individual founded the *Wall Street Journal* and along with Edward Jones created a stock market index that was first calculated in 1896?

28. Lucius Tarquinius Superbus was the last person to hold what title? His reign ended in 509 BC.

29. Following the death of Genghis Khan, who succeeded him to become the second Great Khan of the Mongol Empire?

30. In the quite unexpectedly late year of 1826, when Cayetano Ripoll was hanged in Valencia, he became what is thought to be the last victim of which historical institution?

HISTORY POST-1900

1. Hermann Göring, Joachim von Ribbentrop and Wilhelm Keitel were among those sentenced to death following trials in which city?

2. Since 1900, which comet has been visible twice from earth, in 1910 and in 1986?

3. What was adopted as the national anthem of the United States in 1931?

4. Which company was founded in 1976 by Steve Jobs, Steve Wozniak and Ronald Wayne?

5. In 1980, which infectious disease became the first illness to become successfully eradicated globally?

6. Which nightclub owner shot and murdered Lee Harvey Oswald?

7. Frederick Banting, Charles Best and J J R Macleod first discovered which peptide hormone in 1921?

8. Which aviation pioneer, who was the first female to fly solo across the Atlantic Ocean, disappeared in 1939 during an attempt to make a circumnavigational flight of the globe?

9. Which 1969 music festival began with a performance by Richie Havens?

10. In December 1988, 270 people were killed after Pan Am flight 103 fell over which Scottish town?

11. Which former Prime Minister of the United Kingdom was honoured with the title Earl of Avon?

12. In which city was Martin Luther King Jr assassinated?

13. Born in 1978, the Englishwoman Louise Brown is notable for what reason?

14. Which pioneer of British nursing was executed in 1915 for assisting Allied soldiers in escaping German-occupied Belgium?

15. Rudolf Hess served a life sentence at which prison in West Berlin?

16. The two self-proclaimed People's Republics that are fighting for independence from Ukraine are the Donetsk PR and which other?

17. The acronym MAD refers to which doctrine of military strategy that was a key component of Cold War policy?

18. The Carnation Revolution led to the fall of the authoritarian Estado Novo regime of which country in 1974?

19. Caused by the assassination of Senator Benigno Aquino Jr, the People Power Revolution (Yellow Revolution) saw the overthrow and exile of which Filipino dictator president?

20. The accords of 1995 that put an end to the Bosnian conflict are named for which city in Ohio?

21. Which Irish poet wrote 'Easter, 1916' describing his torn emotions about the events of the Easter Rising and 'September 1, 1939' written during the outbreak of World War Two?

22. Which declaration of 1917 by the British government announced the support of a home for the Jewish people in Palestine?

23. In 1984, which small nation became the last European country to grant women the right to vote?

24. FRELIMO is the dominant political party in which African country?

25. A person who goes by the presumed pseudonymous name Satoshi Nakamoto is best known as the original developer of what?

26. Leon Trotsky was assassinated in which country?

27. An iconic 1937 Picasso work was painted in response to the bombing of which town in the Basque Country?

28. The codename for the naval phase of the Allied Invasion of Normandy shares its name with which planet?

29. At the 2003 UN General Assembly, which US Secretary of State famously held up a test tube that he claimed contained anthrax, citing this as evidence that Iraq was developing WMDs?

30. The 1936 photo 'The Migrant Mother', which has long been associated with the Great Depression, was taken by whom?

LITERATURE 1

1. Kronborg castle in the Danish town of Helsingør was immortalized as Elsinore in which famous work of literature?

2. The 17th-century poet Matsuo Bashō is widely regarded as the greatest master of which poetic form that typically consists of 17 syllables arranged in a 5-7-5 pattern?

3. The sinking of the Nantucket whaling ship *Essex* by a bull sperm whale in 1820 inspired which classic 1851 novel?

4. By what name are Olga, Masha and Irina collectively known in the title of a play by Chekhov?

5. *So Long, and Thanks for All the Fish* is the title of the fourth instalment in which popular series of books?

6. Which best-selling author of *The Pelican Brief* and *The Client* was formerly a lawyer who served in the Mississippi House of Representatives between 1983 and 1990?

7. Which English word was created by John Milton as the name of the capital of Hell in *Paradise Lost*?

8. All the action in which famous novel takes place in Dublin on 16 June 1904?

9. In the poem 'The Raven' by Edgar Allen Poe, which word is repeatedly spoken by the titular bird?

10. In which classic French novel does Rodolphe Boulanger seduce the title character?

11. Famous for her love poems written to other women, the Greek poet Sappho lived and worked on which island?

12. Awarded the 2015 Man Booker Prize, *A Brief History of Seven Killings* by Jamaican author Marlon James tells the story of the attempted assassination of which musician?

13. Which character from Greek myth was 'bound' in the title of a play by Aeschylus and 'unbound' in the title of a poem by Shelley?

14. What is the title of Oscar Wilde's only novel?

15. In which language did Samuel Beckett originally write his play *Waiting for Godot?*

16. Which animal is described as a 'Wee, sleekit, cow'rin, tim'rous beastie' in a poem by Robert Burns?

17. The fictional Long Island towns of West Egg and East Egg are featured in which classic Jazz Age novel?

18. The title of which 1953 sci-fi novel references the temperature at which paper catches fire?

19. Which famous Russian novel opens with the sentence 'All happy families are alike; each unhappy family is unhappy in its own way'?

20. Which novel by Virginia Woolf shares its title with a city in Florida?

21. How is the island of Ireland referred to in the title of a 1904 play by George Bernard Shaw?

22. From the German for 'education novel', what name is given to a novel that focuses on the psychological and moral growth of the protagonist?

23. Which author won the 1921 Pulitzer Prize for Fiction for her novel *The Age of Innocence*, making her the first woman to take the award?

24. In which 20th-century novel would you find cows called Aimless, Feckless, Graceless and Pointless?

25. A 1654 painting by Carel Fabritius of which species of bird inspired a 2013 Pulitzer Prize-winning novel by Donna Tartt?

26. Who wrote the novel *Peyton Place?*

27. Written by David Lagercrantz in 2015, what is the title of the fourth instalment in the *Millennium* series, begun by Stieg Larsson?

28. Aldous Huxley's *Brave New World* tells of the world in the seventh century AF. For what do the letters 'AF' stand?

29. Which Émile Zola novel is named after a month of the French revolutionary calendar?

30. The fictional city of Derry in Maine is the setting for many novels by which author?

LITERATURE 2

1. Which wife of King Henry VIII, his second, is executed at the end of Hilary Mantel's novel *Bring Up the Bodies*?

2. Which novel by George Eliot was first published under the title *The Weaver of Raveloe*?

3. What is the name of the titular Bogeyman in the 1977 picture book created by Raymond Briggs?

4. What is the name of the submarine commanded by Captain Nemo in the Jules Verne story *20,000 Leagues under the Sea*?

5. The Alfred Hitchcock films *Rebecca*, *The Birds* and *Jamaica Inn* were all based on works by which author?

6. In the biblical gospel of St John, what miracle was performed by Jesus at Siloam, a pool near Jerusalem?

7. What is the four-word title of the first novel in James Patterson's Alex Cross series? It's taken from the nursery rhyme 'Little Miss Muffet'.

8. Alex Delarge is the central character of which dystopian novel by Anthony Burgess, published in 1962?

9. 'It was a queer, sultry summer, the summer they electrocuted the Rosenbergs, and I didn't know what I was doing in New York.' This is the opening line of which 1963 novel, originally published by its author under the pseudonym Victoria Lucas?

10. What is the title of the 2017 début novel by Sally Rooney that was made into a television series starring Joe Alwyn and Alison Oliver by Hulu/BBC 3?

11. 'We are all in the gutter but some of us are looking at the stars' is a line from *Lady Windermere's Fan*, written by which author?

12. Which of the Brontë sisters wrote *A Book of Rhymes* when she was just 13? This tiny manuscript sold for just under £1 million in April 2022.

13. Which American writer and activist, the first National Youth Poet Laureate, recited her poem 'The Hill We Climb' at the inauguration of President Joe Biden?

14. Which non-title character speaks the most lines in a single Shakespeare play?

15. The estate of Ian Fleming chose which author to continue writing the James Bond series of books? He has written *Trigger Mortis* (2015), *Forever and a Day* (2018) and *With a Mind to Kill* (2022).

16. How many women feature in the title of the 2019 *New York Times* bestseller written by Lisa Taddeo?

17. According to the title of a 1921 play by Luigi Pirandello, what are The Father, The Mother, The Son, The Stepdaughter, The Boy and The Child in search of?

18. Which work by Simone de Beauvoir was published in two volumes: *Facts and Myths* and *Lived Experience*?

19. Obelix the delivery man is the best friend of which title character in a comic-book series about a village of Gaulish warriors?

20. Which South African author won the Booker Prize in 1974 for her novel *The Conservationist*? She was awarded the Nobel Prize for Literature in 1991.

21. *The Candy House* is a companion novel to, and features characters from, which 2011 Pulitzer Prize-winning work by Jennifer Egan?

22. In the Charles Dickens novel *Oliver Twist*, by what name is the character Jack Dawkins otherwise known?

23. Which writer, born Marguerite Johnson, wrote the autobiographical works *I Know Why the Caged Bird Sings* and *Even the Stars Look Lonesome?*

24. The *Guru Granth Sahib* is the holy book of which religion?

25. Jean Louise Finch, the narrator of Harper Lee's novel *To Kill a Mockingbird*, is also known by what nickname?

26. Nick Carraway is the narrator of which 1925 novel by F Scott Fitzgerald?

27. What is the name of the series of books by Arthur Ransome that centres on the Walker and Blackett families?

28. Which Athenian historian and general is perhaps best remembered for his *History of the Peloponnesian Wars* between Athens and Sparta?

29. In the novel *Harry Potter and the Deathly Hallows*, the Deathly Hallows are the Elder Wand, the Cloak of Invisibility and which other object?

30. *Birthday Letters*, the last major poetry collection published by Ted Hughes, was a study of his relationship with his estranged first wife. What was her name?

MYTHOLOGY

1. What is the name of the king of the gods in Roman mythology, after whom the largest planet in the solar system is named?

2. What is the name of the castle that was home to the court of King Arthur?

3. Aphrodite is the goddess of what in Greek mythology? Venus is her counterpart in Roman mythology.

4. Which forest is said to have been the home of Robin Hood and his Merry Men?

5. Which mythological creature with a large, spiralling horn projecting from its forehead is the national animal of Scotland?

6. Legendary marksman William Tell is considered a national hero of which European country?

7. What is the name of the ship on which Jason and his band of heroes set out to recover the Golden Fleece?

8. The stories of 'Aladdin', 'Ali Baba and the 40 Thieves' and 'Sinbad the Sailor' are most closely associated with which collection of Middle Eastern folktales?

9. Leaving what item at the gates of the city of Troy led to the creation of the phrase 'beware of Greeks bearing gifts'?

10. In Irish folklore, which female spirits herald the death of a family member by wailing or shrieking?

11. In Norse mythology, Bifröst, the bridge guarded by the god Heimdall that connects Midgard, the realm of man, and Asgard, the realm of the gods, was made up of what kind of meteorological phenomenon?

12. Although he is better known in Greek mythology as being the god of something else, which major god is also the god of horses?

13. What kind of weapon was Mjolnir, which was wielded by the Norse god of thunder Thor?

14. In the story of Beowulf, what is the name of the monster he slays in the Hall of King Hrothgar after tearing its arm from its body?

15. What is the traditional occupation of leprechauns in Irish folklore?

16. What part of the Underworld in Greek mythology was reserved for people who had been judged to have been wicked and had to be punished for eternity?

17. Taken in 1934, 'The Surgeon's Photograph' supposedly features what mythical creature?

18. The brothers Castor and Pollux from Greek mythology are depicted in the Zodiac as what star sign?

19. The last of Heracles' 12 Labours involved having to capture what three-headed dog?

20. What was the answer to the Riddle of the Sphinx in Greek mythology?

21. In Greek mythology who was the mother of the winged horse Pegasus?

22. Bjorn Ironside, Sigurd Snake in His Eye and Ivar the Boneless were all sons of which legendary Viking king?

23. Zeus was a great admirer of which figure from Greek mythology until he was put off by the prophecy that her son would be greater than his father? As a result, she was married off to Peleus and became the mother of Achilles.

24. What quiz-related word was the name of the first man created by the gods in Norse mythology?

25. On what island was the Labyrinth, in which Theseus killed the minotaur?

26. The mythical figure Jimmu is credited as being the first person to hold what title, which is still used by the head of state of a modern-day country?

27. Which was the only animal in Chinese mythology that failed to finish the race that was used to determine the animals the years were named for and, as a result, doesn't have a year named after it?

28. For lusting after Zeus' wife Hera while a guest of Zeus at Mount Olympus, which figure in Greek mythology was punished by being bound to a winged fiery wheel that spun for all eternity?

29. Which legendary King of Rome is said to have disappeared in a whirlwind during a sudden violent storm while reviewing his troops and was never seen again?

30. In Egyptian mythology the god Horus had the head of what kind of bird?

PHYSICS

1. Sharing its name with one of the world's largest car rental companies, what is the SI unit of frequency?

2. What English scientist's first law of motion is also known as the law of inertia?

3. What name given to the positively charged central core of an atom is also used to describe the part of an animal or plant cell that contains genetic material?

4. Absolute zero is to be found on which temperature scale named after a British scientist born in 1824?

5. In Einstein's famous equation $E = mc^2$, what is denoted by the letter c?

6. Named after an Austrian physicist, the apparent change of frequency in a sound wave perceived by an observer as the source of the sound passes by is known as what?

7. Often found in science labs at schools, what is an electrostatic machine that uses a moving belt to accumulate very high voltages on a hollow metal globe better known as?

8. The German scientist Wilhelm Röntgen won the first-ever Nobel Prize in Physics for his discovery of what?

9. Discovered experimentally by Otto Hahn, what name is given to a nuclear reaction in which the nucleus of an atom splits into two smaller and lighter nuclei?

10. All subatomic particles can be split into two groups. The bosons are named after an Indian physicist, but which Italian physicist gives his name to the other group?

11. The opposite of an anion, what name is given to an ion that has an excess of protons compared with electrons and, therefore, has a positive charge?

12. In optics, Snell's law governs the relationship between angle of incidence and what process whereby a wave changes its direction passing from one medium to another?

13. What is the two-word term for the speed attained by an object when the sum of the drag force and the buoyancy is equal to the downward force of gravity acting on it?

14. In quantum mechanics, what name is given to the amount of angular momentum associated with a subatomic particle?

15. Which 19th-century Scottish physicist formulated a set of equations which proved that electricity and magnetism were two aspects of the same force?

16. Dividing mass by volume will give you which property, often abbreviated by the lower-case Greek letter rho?

17. What name is given to the field of mechanics concerned with the launching, flight behaviour and impact effects of projectiles?

18. Up, down, charm, strange, top and bottom are the six 'flavours' of which type of elementary particle?

19. In astrophysics, what does a star become when it collapses to a radius less than the Schwarzchild limit?

20. Which British physicist won the Royal Society's 2015 Copley Medal for his work in theorizing the existence of his namesake boson?

21. Which Austrian physicist gives his name to the Exclusion Principle, which states that no two identical fermions may simultaneously occupy the same quantum state?

22. Discovered by French physicist Paul Villard in 1900, which form of electromagnetic radiation has the shortest wavelength?

23. Which astronomic unit of measurement is equal to 3.26 light years?

24. Also known as moment of force, rotational force or turning effect, what is the rotational equivalent of linear force?

25. Quantum theory is commonly held to have been formulated in 1900 by which German physicist when he provided a solution to the black-body radiation problem?

26. Albert Einstein won the Nobel Prize in Physics in 1921 for his explanation of which observation that many metals emit electrons when light shines upon them?

27. In physics, what term is used for a loop of wire, often wrapped around a metallic core, that produces a magnetic field when an electric current is passed through it?

28. In physics, what name is given to the measure of the unavailable energy in a closed thermodynamic system, and is often described as the measure of the system's disorder?

29. Which subatomic particle is the quantum of electromagnetic radiation and, thus, the most basic unit of light?

30. Which two-word term is used to describe the gravitational boundary enclosing a black hole, from which nothing can escape?

POLITICS

1. The heads of four American Presidents are carved into Mount Rushmore in South Dakota. If Abraham Lincoln, Thomas Jefferson and Theodore Roosevelt are three, who is the fourth?

2. In December 2021, Olaf Scholz succeeded which individual as Chancellor of Germany? She had held the role from 2005 to 2021.

3. After the overthrow of the US-backed Fulgencio Batista, who became the leader of Cuba in 1959? He ruled until 2008, when he handed over power to his brother Raul.

4. What is the name given to the transcripts of parliamentary debates in Britain and other Commonwealth countries? It is the surname of Luke and his son Thomas, who first printed these accounts.

5. Karine Jean-Pierre replaced Jen Psaki to become the first Black, openly gay holder of which office in the White House?

6. Who replaced Harold Wilson as Prime Minister of the United Kingdom when he resigned in April 1976?

7. What is the two-word metonym used to describe the United States Department of State, named for its low-lying, marshy riverside location in Washington DC?

8. In May 2022, Anthony Albanese became the first Labour Prime Minister of which country since Kevin Rudd in 2013?

9. Who is the only person to become President of the United States without being elected either President or Vice-President?

10. Which world leader did French President François Mitterrand describe as having 'the eyes of Caligula and the mouth of Marilyn Monroe'?

11. According to Article II of the US Constitution, a President of the USA must be a minimum of what age?

12. Under what name did the military leader born Arthur Wellesley serve as British Prime Minister between 1828 and 1830 and then again in 1834?

13. According to its first Secretary General, Hastings Ismay, which organization was created to 'keep the Russians out, the Americans in and the Germans down'?

14. Which American President was nominated to the Supreme Court eight years after his one-term presidency?

15. Which current Prime Minister, the 23rd to hold that role in his country, has a father who was the 15th Prime Minister of the same country?

16. Who is the only leader of the UK Labour party to serve three separate terms in three different decades – the 1900s, 1910s and 1930s?

17. In 2021 Christian Smalls became the founder and first leader of a labour union at which international e-commerce retailer?

18. Elected in 1997, Jenny Shipley was both the first leader of the National Party and the first female Prime Minister of which Commonwealth country?

19. Who was both the first American President to be born an American citizen and also the first who did not speak English as his first language?

20. In May 2022, who did Emmanuel Macron appoint as the second female Prime Minister of France?

21. Who was appointed as the Chief Executive of Hong Kong in July 2017? She relinquished the role in July 2022.

22. One of the longest-ruling non-royal leaders in the world, which former revolutionary has served as President of Nicaragua since 2007?

23. What is the name of the bicameral legislature of the Federal government of the United States that meets in the Capitol building and that comprises the Senate and the House of Representatives?

24. Replacing Rodrigo Duterte, what is the nickname of Ferdinand Marcos Jr, the President of the Philippines, who took office in June 2022?

25. The first two women to be Presidents of Ireland had the surnames Robinson and McAleese and shared what forename?

26. Which American President, assassinated by Charles Guiteau in 1881, was a noted polymath who could write Ancient Greek with one hand and at the same time classical Latin with the other?

27. Kamala Harris, the first female Vice-President of the United States, served as Attorney General and a Senator for which state between 2011 and 2021?

28. The Republic of Artsakh forms part of which region that is the subject of a long-running political dispute between Armenia and Azerbaijan?

29. Which United Nations Secretary General served only one term in the role, between 1992 and 1996, after the United States vetoed his second term?

30. Two British Prime Ministers were born outside the British Isles. The first was Andrew Bonar Law, who was the second?

POP MUSIC PRE-2000

1. Which chart topper shares his name with a character from *Scooby Doo?*

2. Which two questions are asked in the opening lyrics to 'Bohemian Rhapsody'?

3. Which guitarist played 'The Star-Spangled Banner' at the 1969 Woodstock Festival?

4. Which Billy Joel song mentions more than 50 famous people from the 20th century?

5. Who staged a sing-along at Wimbledon when it started to rain in 1996?

6. Which nightclub was located at 10 Mathew Street, in Liverpool?

7. Marti Pellow was the singer of which group?

8. In which decade was the first edition of *Smash Hits* published?

9. In which year were the following songs at number three, number two and number one – 'There Goes My First Love', 'The Last Farewell' and 'Barbados'?

10. Formed in Woking, Surrey, which pop group had three singles go straight into the charts at number one in the 1980s?

11. Backstreet Boys, Joe South, Janet Kay and Peter Gabriel have all had top ten hit singles with which word in the song title?

12. Which Peter Gabriel song references the TV show *It's a Knockout?*

13. Cindy Birdsong replaced Florence Ballard in which all-girl group in 1967?

14. The short-lived National Centre for Popular Music opened in which city in 1999, closing in 2000?

15. What is the name of the Undertones' 'perfect cousin', according to the lyrics of the song?

16. Complete the title of this 1988 track by REM – 'Orange…'?

17. Which Phil Collins song was track one, on side one, of the compilation album *Now That's What I Call Music*, also known as *Now 1*?

18. What colour was the sea in the Beatles' song 'Yellow Submarine'?

19. Prince won an Oscar for his music for which film?

20. Which famous singer formed the group Tin Machine in 1989?

21. Who was the only female solo artist to have two UK number one singles in the 1970s?

22. Roy Orbison was the first Roy to have a UK top 40 hit single. Who was the second?

23. Which country links Kraftwerk and Bonnie Tyler?

24. Which musical instruments did ABC hear 'When Smokey Sings'?

25. Who has had hits with Sir Paul McCartney, Michael Jackson, Dionne Warwick, Julio Iglesias and Babyface?

26. Which radio station began broadcasting on 28 March 1964?

27. Kool & the Gang and Gina G have both had top ten hit singles with which one-word title?

28. Who did the Sutherland Brothers want to lie in the arms of?

29. Which duo's Christian names are Daryl and John?

30. 'Dub Be Good to Me', a number one hit single for Beats International, was a reworking of 'Just Be Good to Me', a song by which American group?

POP MUSIC POST-2000

1. Which card game features in the title of one of Lady Gaga's first songs to top the charts?

2. 'I heard that you're settled down, that you found a girl and you're married now' are the opening lyrics to which Adele song?

3. Since 2003, any wedding, party or disco would be incomplete without which song by The Killers, the first single they ever released?

4. Which British boy band made a comeback with the song 'Patience' in 2006?

5. Which ancient city gives its name to one of Bastille's biggest hits?

6. Thanks to its use in the Netflix series *Stranger Things*, which song by Kate Bush reached its highest-ever peak in the summer of 2022?

7. Who is the first woman to have won three Album of the Year Awards at the Grammys? She picked up the third of the three in 2021 with *folklore*.

8. The film *8 Mile* contained the song 'Lose Yourself' and catapulted which rapper to mainstream success?

9. Wiley is credited as one of the founders of which genre of rap music that Stormzy and Dave helped to popularize?

10. 'Seven Nation Army', a song now often used in sporting chants, reached the top ten in the UK for which rock duo?

11. The Nottingham couple Mark and Roxanne Hoyle are known by which stage name? They have achieved a record number of back-to-back Christmas number ones.

12. What is the name of the drummer for Blink-182? Known as one of the greatest drummers of all time, he got engaged to Kourtney Kardashian in October 2021.

13. 'Long live life' is the English translation of which song by Coldplay?

14. 'Shotgun' and 'Budapest' were both huge hits for which English singer?

15. The Canadian rock band Nickelback wished that they had a bathroom they could play baseball in, as well as many other luxuries, in which hit song?

16. Which artist's debut studio album was *I Created Disco*? Since then, he has worked with Rihanna on the song 'We Found Love' and Florence Welch on 'Sweet Nothing'.

17. Which English singer and songwriter claims in her song 'The Fear' that doesn't care about clever or funny, she just wants to be rich?

18. 'Old Town Road', featuring Billy Ray Cyrus, was the song that put which American rapper on the map?

19. A cover version of which song features on the soundtrack of *Donnie Darko*? It was recorded for the film by Michael Andrews and Gary Jules.

20. 'Good 4 U' and 'Drivers License' are both songs from which ex-Disney singer's album *Sour*?

21. Madcon and Måneskin both had chart success with which song?

22. Childish Gambino is the stage name of which American rapper? He is also famous for stand-up comedy and acting.

23. Which was the first mathematical symbol to grace the cover of an Ed Sheeran album? The album in question includes the songs 'Lego House' and 'The A Team'.

24. In a number one song from 2005, which artist wished that they were a punk rocker with flowers in their hair?

25. Jack Harlow's hit 'First Class' samples which 2007 song by Fergie that features Ludacris?

26. 'Say So', 'Streets' and 'Kiss Me More' are all hits from which American rapper?

27. 'Chaise Longue' and 'Ur Mum' are both songs from which British indie band's eponymous album, which debuted at number one?

28. What is the title of the song for which the Kalush Orchestra won the 2022 Eurovision song contest with a record number of public votes?

29. Alfred Yankovic is the real name of which American singer who is known for his humorous parodies of pop songs?

30. 'Without You 'and 'Stay' are both hits by which Australian rapper? 'Stay' was a collaboration with Justin Bieber.

RELIGION

1. In the Bible, St Paul was on the road to which city when he was blinded by the light and converted to Christianity?

2. What is the name of the hemispherical or platter-shaped skullcap, usually of cloth, often worn by Orthodox Jewish men to fulfil the customary requirement that their heads be covered at all times?

3. By what name are monks of the Order of the Reformed Cistercians of the Strict Observance, noted for their austerity of diet and absolute silence, usually known?

4. Born in Tibet in 1935, Tenzin Gyatso is the current holder of which religious title?

5. Islam's holiest site is which building in Mecca that serves as the destination of those performing the Hajj?

6. In which African country was the Coptic Church founded in the first century AD?

7. Celebrated on 8 April, Hanamatsuri is a Japanese flower festival marking the birth of which major spiritual leader, born in what is now Nepal in the fifth or sixth century B C ?

8. According to the Bible, in which garden was Jesus betrayed by Judas?

9. The surname Singh, commonly used by Sikhs, is an ancient Indian name for which animal?

10. Which country is home to the world's largest Muslim population?

11. In which river did John the Baptist perform the baptism of Jesus?

12. What is the name of the headscarf often worn by Muslim women that covers the head and neck but leaves the face clear, unlike the niqab or the burqa?

13. In which trade were Simon Peter and his brother Andrew working when Jesus called them to follow him?

14. Also known as the Day of Atonement, what is the Hebrew name of the holiest day of the year in Judaism?

15. Often observed as a rest day in many parts of the Islamic world, which day of the week is holy to Muslims?

16. Which ancient religion is based on the teachings of Mahavira, a holy man born in India in the sixth century BC?

17. Saraswati, the Hindu goddess of arts and learning, is said to have invented which ancient language?

18. Recently popular with celebrities, what is the name of the ancient Jewish esoteric tradition of mystical interpretation of scripture?

19. Which modern Pagan religion, sometimes called Pagan witchcraft, was developed in England and introduced to the public by Gerald Gardner in 1954?

20. Which seven-lamp candelabrum has served as a symbol of Judaism since ancient times? A nine-lamp candelabrum of the same name is also used at Hanukkah.

21. Usually painted vermillion, a torii is a gate that marks the entrance to a shrine in which religion?

22. What was the name of the church founded in Korea in 1954 by the Reverend Sun Myung Moon, whose adherents are sometimes called Moonies?

23. What is the is the first word in the Qur'an? It also appears three times in the lyrics of Queen's 'Bohemian Rhapsody'.

24. One of the most important figures in Hindu scripture, Hanuman is said to have led an army of which animals into battle against the demonic King Ravana?

25. Which musical instrument, traditionally made from a ram's horn, is blown at certain Jewish religious ceremonies?

26. Fire temples, almost a third of which are found in Mumbai, are places of worship for members of which religion?

27. Which emblem of St James is traditionally worn by pilgrims to the Spanish city of Santiago de Compostela?

28. Which important figure in Taoist history and thought is said to have been conceived when his mother gazed upon a falling star?

29. Literally meaning 'avoidance of violence', which central tenet of Jainism, which is also found in Hinduism and Buddhism, bars the killing or injuring of living beings?

30. What is the name of the diet followed by many Rastafarians? Following this diet is compulsory in the Nyabinghi Mansion, this religion's oldest branch.

SPORT 1

1. There are three Grand Tours in the sport of cycling. La Vuelta a España and the Giro d'Italia are two, which is the third?

2. The phrase 'hook, line and sinker', meaning to be taken in by something, originates in which hugely popular participation sport?

3. What is the name of the annual best-of-three series of rugby league matches in Australia, between New South Wales and Queensland?

4. Which Denver Nuggets player was named NBA Most Valuable Player (MVP) of the season in both 2021 and 2022?

5. George Lyon won the men's golf gold medal at the 1904 Summer Olympic Games. Which Englishman was the next winner of that gold medal at the 2016 Summer Olympics?

6. What is the nationality of golfer Mito Pereira, whose double-bogey on the last hole of the 2022 USPGA cost him his first major title in only his second-ever major championship?

7. Two of the fastest goals ever scored in the English Premier League were scored by Ledley King and Christian Eriksen, who were both playing for which team at the time they scored?

8. In 1983, who was the last Frenchman to win the men's singles at the French Open Tennis Championship? This player's son went on to have a career as a basketball player in the NBA in the United States.

9. At the 2022 Winter Olympics, the women's and men's gold medals in which team sport were won by Canada and Finland?

10. Which West Indian batsman scored 214 and 100 not out in the two innings of his début Test match against New Zealand in 1972?

11. Winning two gold, one silver and five bronze medals, who is Britain's most decorated female athlete at the World Athletics Championship?

12. Which French team won its eighth Women's Football Champions League title, beating Barcelona in the 2022 final?

13. Which Canadian darts player is a three-time World Champion, beating Bobby George, Phil Taylor and Kirk Shepherd to win those finals?

14. The only player to win the FIH Player of the Year Award on eight occasions, Luciana Aymar of Argentina is often described as the world's greatest-ever female player of which sport?

15. The Laureus World Sports Awards were first held in the year 2000. Which Spanish golfer won the Breakthrough Award at the first awards ceremony in 2000?

16. What first name and surname are shared by the captain of the Welsh team that won the 2005 rugby union Six Nations grand slam and the only England footballer to score goals in four consecutive tournaments?

17. Which boxer, nicknamed 'the Executioner', defeated Jean Pascal to become light heavyweight World Champion in 2011 at the age of 46, making him the oldest World Champion in boxing history?

18. Ken Griffey Jr began and ended his professional baseball career, in which he hit 630 home runs, with which team?

19. Who made history in 2021 when riding Minella Times to become the first female jockey to win the Aintree Grand National?

20. The Weber Cup, competed for by Team Europe and Team USA since the year 2000, is an annual competition in which sport?

21. What is the name of the annual match between the nine-ball pool teams representing Team Europe and Team USA?

22. The American athlete Ed Moses won 122 consecutive races between 1977 and 1987 in which track event?

23. The unofficial triple crown of motor sport consists of the Indianapolis 500, the Le Mans 24 Hour race and which Formula One grand prix, which was first held in 1929?

24. When *Forbes* magazine ranked the highest-paid sportspeople in the world between May 2021 and May 2022, four of the top ten were competitors in which sport?

25. Which team lost four American Football Superbowls in 1970, 1973, 1974 and 1977? These are the only occasions on which the team ever reached the Superbowl.

26. Which Brazilian mixed martial artist, the first woman to become a two-weight UFC Champion, defeated Cris Cyborg to win the world featherweight title in 2018?

27. At the 2012 London Olympics, who became the first African-American woman to win a gymnastics gold medal in the individual all-around competition?

28. Which nation, represented by Janette Husarova and Daniela Hantuchova, won their only tennis Fed Cup (now the Billie Jean King Cup) in 2002, by beating Spain 3-1 in the final?

29. In Turkey, the Intercontinental Derby is a fiercely contested and supported football match between Fenerbahçe and which other team?

30. Nicknamed 'the Rocket', which snooker player won his seventh world title in 2022, beating Judd Trump in the final?

SPORT 2

1. What five-letter word does the golfer Eldrick Woods typically use instead of his first name?

2. The English soccer teams Manchester United and Liverpool and the American football teams the San Francisco 49ers and Kansas City Chiefs play their home games in shirts of mainly what colour?

3. How many points is the bullseye worth in a game of darts?

4. Which athlete won the men's 100m and 200m in track and field at the 2008, 2012 and 2016 Summer Olympics?

5. Which country's two victories in the FIFA Men's World Cup came in 1998 and 2018?

6. When a batter in cricket is given out without scoring any runs, they are said to have scored what kind of bird?

7. Basketball player Magic Johnson spent his entire playing career at which NBA team?

8. When Lewis Hamilton won his seventh Formula One World Championship, he equalled which other driver's record for the most Formula One Championships?

9. Before moving to Los Angeles, the major league baseball team the Dodgers were based in which borough of New York City?

10. In which city does the cycling race the Giro d'Italia finish each year?

11. Which Australian horse race is known as 'the race that stops the nation'?

12. Which is event is combined with cross-country skiing at the Winter Olympics to make up the biathlon event?

13. When a person taps out in an MMA or wrestling bout, what are they indicating they are doing?

14. The two disciplines of Olympic weightlifting are the snatch and which other style of lift?

15. Which tennis player won the ladies singles Championship at Wimbledon every year between 1982 and 1987?

16. Which of the Olympic swimming strokes is the slowest?

17. When the balls are set up at the start of a frame of snooker, which colour ball is placed on the spot at the centre of the table?

18. Who did the Green Bay Packers beat in 1967 to win the first-ever Superbowl?

19. What is the only non-European location to have hosted two Winter Olympics?

20. Muhammad Ali won his first World Heavyweight Boxing Championship when he beat which boxer in 1964?

21. The Borg-Warner Trophy is awarded every year to the winner of which annual American sporting event?

22. When entering the ring, the wrestler Jake Roberts would carry what kind of reptile ring with him? He would later place this animal on knocked-out opponents.

23. What nickname is given to the American footballer who is drafted in last place in the annual NFL Draft?

24. Every year between 2016 and 2022, both the men's and women's Squash World Champions came from which country?

25. Seemiller, shakehand and penhold are all ways of gripping your playing equipment in which sport?

26. Which city is the home of the annual middle-distance track race the Dream Mile? It also hosts the Bislett Games.

27. Who is the only basketball player to win the Most Valuable Player award in both the American Basketball Association and the National Basketball Association?

28. Meaning 'grand champion', what is the highest rank a competitor can achieve in sumo wrestling?

29. Between 1995 and 2005, the Austrian soccer team Sturm Graz played at a stadium named after which person who was born nearby?

30. Despite not having been very successful in the men's game, which country's team won the first Women's Rugby Union World Cup?

SPORT 3

1. What is the surname of the boxer known as 'Iron Mike' or 'The Baddest Man on the Planet'?

2. Which sporting trophy was hidden under the bed of Ottorino Barassi, the Italian Vice-President of FIFA, during World War Two?

3. How many players are there on a polo team?

4. Who directed the opening ceremony of the 2012 Olympic Games?

5. Who was Steve Redgrave's partner in his Olympic Games victories in the coxless pairs rowing event in 1992 and 1996?

6. Which player went on loan from Spurs to Paris Saint-Germain for much of the 1982–83 season due to the Falklands War?

7. What scores three points in rugby union, but only one point in rugby league?

8. All five Irish horse racing classics are held at which racecourse?

9. What is the name given to the annual T20 competition held in Australia?

10. Which Formula One team has their headquarters in Woking, Surrey?

11. Darts player Anastasia Dobromyslova shares her nickname with which James Bond film?

12. Who was the first European to play in and captain winning Ryder Cup teams?

13. What name is shared by a 1960s band fronted by Andy Fairweather Low and a series of three holes at Augusta Golf Course?

14. What shape is the ring used in the UFC (Ultimate Fighting Championship)?

15. Which famous sporting trophy was badly damaged by a Maori protester in 1997?

16. Which yachtswoman began saving her school dinner money at the age of eight to buy a boat?

17. In cricket, what are the fielding positions next to the wicketkeeper on the off side called?

18. Kornelia Ender won eight Olympic medals in which sport?

19. In what game would a player use their 'squidger' to shoot a small plastic disc into a target?

20. Tennis player Vijay Amritraj made a cameo appearance in which James Bond film?

21. The 2013 Tour de France started on which Mediterranean island?

22. Which sport featured in the film *White Men Can't Jump*?

23. What caused the Cheltenham Gold Cup to be postponed in 2001?

24. Which winter sport has a boundary known as the hog line?

25. On which motor racing circuit would you find the Hanger Straight and Chapel Curve?

26. In which sport is a ball with double yellow spots extra slow and a blue spot fast?

27. The Lions, Tigers, Pistons and Red Wings are sporting teams in which US city?

28. Francois Pienaar played rugby union for which country?

29. Irish boxer Steve Collins defeated which English fighter to win the WBO super-middleweight title?

30. The 2018 World Cup squad of which country included Thomas Delaney and Martin Braithwaite?

TV

1. What is the name of the starship that provided the main setting for both the original *Star Trek* TV series and *Star Trek: The Next Generation?*

2. Which 1990s TV show centred on the lives of the lifeguards who patrolled the beaches of Los Angeles County?

3. The TV shows *Stranger Things*, *The Crown*, *Bridgerton* and *Cobra Kai* can all be found on what streaming service?

4. What is the first name of Homer and Marge's oldest daughter in *The Simpsons?*

5. The Starks, the Lannisters, the Targaryens and the Greyjoys are all noble houses in which fantasy TV series?

6. The British version of which sitcom was set in Slough, the German version in Cologne, the French in Villepinte and the American version in Scranton, Pennsylvania?

7. The TV series *M*A*S*H* is set during which war? The TV series was on the air for 11 years, which is 8 years longer than the war lasted.

8. *Droids*, *The Clone Wars* and *Rebels* are all animated TV series featuring characters from which film franchise?

9. Robert Crawley, Hugh Bonneville's character in *Downton Abbey*, is the earl of which English town?

10. What was the first name of the television detective Kojak?

11. The Cylons are the main antagonists in which science-fiction television series?

12. The TV character Arthur Fonzarelli is better known by what nickname?

13. The title of which TV series based on the activities of Easy Company, a battalion of the 506th Infantry Parachute Regiment in World War Two, comes from the Shakespeare play *Henry V*?

14. Which actress played the title characters in the 1990s TV shows *Clarissa Explains It All* and *Sabrina the Teenage Witch*?

15. After the six main characters in the sitcom *Friends*, which character appeared in the most episodes of the show? The character worked as a barista in Central Perk.

16. In both the British and American versions of *Being Human*, the characters who initially share a house are a ghost, a vampire and what other kind of creature?

17. The cartoon series *Daria* was a spin-off from which other animated series?

18. What was the name of the character played by Phil Silvers in the *Phil Silvers Show*?

19. The entire ninth series of the soap opera *Dallas* was revealed to be a dream when which character woke up and saw the husband she thought was dead taking a shower?

20. Played by Renée O'Connor, Gabrielle was the sidekick of which TV character played by Lucy Lawless?

21. Alex Trebek hosted the quiz show *Jeopardy* from 1984 until his death in 2020, but who was the host of the show from when it first aired in 1964 until 1979?

22. The DC Comics TV series *The Flash*, *Supergirl*, *Legends of Tomorrow*, *Black Lightning* and *Batwoman* are collectively known by what name, which contains the name of the initial series in this franchise?

23. In *Doctor Who*, the Doctor's TARDIS is permanently stuck in the form of a police phone box due to which circuit being broken?

24. Of all the games played in the Netflix series *Squid Game*, which is the only one that has featured in a less deadly form in the Olympic Games?

25. Which future two-time Oscar winner played Dr Phillip Chandler in the medical drama *St. Elsewhere*?

26. The original 1980s version of *Dynasty* was mostly set in Denver. The rebooted version, which started in 2017, instead takes place mainly in which other US city?

27. At the start of the TV series *I, Claudius*, who is the Emperor of Rome?

28. Cactus Head, Outlaw Scuzz, Tex Hex and Stampede are the enemies of which futuristic cartoon lawman who lived on the planet New Texas?

29. A black GMC Vandura was the vehicle of choice for which group of TV characters?

30. What is the name of the fictional country that is the setting for the TV series *The Handmaid's Tale*?

WORDS & LANGUAGE

> *'Here we go, the last one', Mark said before tackling this quiz. 'Could be a tricky subject, this.'*

1. What weather would you expect in France if you heard the phrase *'il pleut'*?

2. In which alphabet would you find letters beta, zeta and theta?

3. Foxtrot is the first dance to appear in the NATO phonetic alphabet. What is the second?

4. What was the surname of the Frenchman who created a reading system for visually impaired people?

5. English and which other language are the two most spoken languages in the world?

6. Assuming no double/triple letter/word spaces are used, what would the word 'quiz' score in a game of Scrabble?

7. 'Shalom', 'todah' and 'ken' ('hello', 'thank you' and 'yes') are common words in which language?

8. Which American author, best known for his travel writing, wrote *Mother Tongue: The Story of the English Language*?

9. Which language is widely regarded as the world's oldest?

10. Starting 'supercali', the magic word from the film *Mary Poppins* contains how many letters?

11. The Latin phrase *'carpe diem'* can be translated as what?

12. According to the antiquated German phrase *'Kinder, Küche, Kirche'*, what are a woman's three roles in society?

13. Widely regarded as England's greatest-ever writer and dramatist, Shakespeare was born in which century?

14. The use of fire, lights or flags to create a visual signal transmitted over distance is known as what?

15. The phrase 'on your jollies' means you are where?

16. What is the most-used word in the Bible?

17. JavaScript, HTML and SQL are common what?

18. In grammar, connecting words such as 'but', 'and' or 'if' are known as what?

19. What is the most-spoken language in Pakistan?

20. What were the first words thought to be spoken on the moon?

21. Old news, working vacation, small crowd, bittersweet, crash landing are all examples of what?

22. Whose autobiography, *The Story of My Life*, detailed her experiences as a deaf and blind person?

23. If you were enjoying goon in Australia, what would you be drinking?

24. The lemniscate symbol is better known by what mathematical term?

25. What is the only English word that begins and ends with the letters 'und'?

26. What is the world's most-translated document?

27. What is the dot over the lowercase letters i or j called?

28. What word meaning the action or process of searching for and publishing private or identifying information about a particular individual on the Internet was added to the *English Oxford Dictionary* in 2021?

29. In English, what is the shortest word that contains the letters 'abcd' and 'f'?

30. Which East Papuan language has, arguably, the smallest alphabet of any language spoken in the world today?

ANSWERS

GENERAL KNOWLEDGE 1 – EASY

	THE BEAST	YOU
1. Sausage rolls	✓	☐
2. *Lord of the Dance*	✓	☐
3. Jason Donovan	✓	☐
4. Uncle	✓	☐
5. Europe	✓	☐
6. *Dad's Army*	✓	☐
7. Coral	✓	☐
8. Arabic	✓	☐
9. Pear	✓	☐
10. Idaho	✓	☐
11. Harvey Wallbanger	✓	☐
12. Aries	✓	☐

> ***Mark: 'April Fools' Day was the Pagan new year. The Pagan calendar predates the Christian one, which is why Aries is the first star sign and Pisces the last.'***

	THE BEAST	YOU
13. 'You'll Never Walk Alone'	✓	☐
14. Equilateral	✓	☐
15. Bristol	✓	☐
16. Khyber Pass	✓	☐
17. Pea green	✓	☐
18. Findus	✓	☐
19. Chickpeas	✓	☐

	THE BEAST	YOU
20. Great Ormond Street Hospital	✓	☐

> *Mark: 'Great Ormond Street Hospital has received millions of pounds in royalties since J M Barrie left the rights of his fairytale to the London hospital before his death in 1937. Copyright normally expires after 70 years, after which works become free for others to use without having to seek permission or pay royalties. However, Peter Pan is an exception. Through a special bill in the UK, the boy who never grows up has been granted a copyright that, at least in part, will never expire.'*

21. A cable	✓	☐
22. The Michelin Man	✓	☐
23. Tuesday	✓	☐
24. Doberman	✓	☐
25. Bed	✓	☐

> *Mark: 'Shakespeare died on his 57th birthday – born and died on St George's Day.'*

26. Sumo wrestling	✓	☐

> *Mark: 'My sumo record is played one and lost one.'*

27. Britney Spears	✓	☐
28. 1963	✓	☐

	THE BEAST	YOU
29. Five farthings	✓	☐
30. Hosanna	✗	☐
SCORE	29/30	___/30

	THE BEAST	YOU
1. Orange	✓	☐
2. 29 February	✓	☐
3. Chicken	✓	☐
4. Guernsey	✓	☐
5. Snakebite	✓	☐
6. Leningrad	✓	☐
7. Peter	✓	☐
8. Quartet	✓	☐
9. Spain	✓	☐
10. Sunday	✓	☐
11. Current	✓	☐

Mark: 'Amperes are used to measure the number of electrons flowing through a circuit: one amp is the amount of current produced by a force of one volt acting through the resistance of one ohm. An ampere is one of the seven fundamentals quantities – the others are kilogram for mass, second for time, kelvin for temperature, mole for the amount of substance, candela for luminous intensity and metre for distance.'

	THE BEAST	YOU
12. Hyacinth	✓	☐
13. Oxfordshire	✗	☐
14. Embossed	✗	☐
15. The Smurfs	✓	☐

	THE BEAST	YOU
16. Foxtrot	✓	☐
17. One million	✓	☐
18. Opal Fruits	✓	☐
19. Othello	✓	☐
20. One in six	✓	☐
21. M25	✓	☐
22. Philippines	✓	☐
23. Octopus	✗	☐
24. P T Barnum	✓	☐
25. Molly Malone	✓	☐
26. Vortex	✗	☐
27. Fitzwilliam	✓	☐
28. Keelhauling	✓	☐
29. Lemmy	✓	☐
30. Mauritania	✗	☐

Mark: 'Under Muammar Gaddafi's dictatorship, Libya had a red, white and black flag from 1969 to 1977. This was replaced by an all-green flag from 1977 to 2011, making it the only flag in the world to have only one colour and no design.'

SCORE 25/30 ___/30

GENERAL KNOWLEDGE 3 – EASY

		THE BEAST	YOU
1.	The A-Team	✓	☐
2.	(Baked) Alaska	✓	☐
3.	Lucius	✓	☐
4.	Bree (Van de Kamp)	✓	☐
5.	*Grease*	✓	☐
6.	Guantanamo Bay	✓	☐
7.	Ian Rush	✓	☐
8.	Juniper	✓	☐

> **Mark:** '*In the early days of the coronavirus pandemic, some gin distilleries announced plans to switch to producing hand sanitizer.*'

		THE BEAST	YOU
9.	Ken Dodd	✓	☐
10.	Rio de Janeiro	✓	☐
11.	Ten	✓	☐
12.	Belfast	✓	☐
13.	Crocus	✓	☐
14.	Glaucoma	✓	☐
15.	Kings of Leon	✓	☐
16.	Griffin	✓	☐
17.	Sleepwalking	✓	☐
18.	Wisconsin	✓	☐
19.	$1.91 ($1 + 50¢ + 25¢ + 10¢ + 5¢ + 1¢)	✗	☐

	THE BEAST	YOU
20. Neurology	✓	☐
21. Offside	✓	☐
22. Harry Ramsden's	✓	☐
23. Russell Brand	✓	☐
24. Scamper	✗	☐
25. Elephant	✓	☐
26. Noah	✓	☐
27. Warrington	✗	☐
28. Leadbeater	✓	☐
29. Finland	✓	☐
30. Derek Nimmo	✓	☐
SCORE	**27/30**	**___/30**

GENERAL KNOWLEDGE 4 – EASY

		THE BEAST	YOU
1.	Greece	✓	☐
2.	Noughts and crosses	✓	☐
3.	Lumbar	✓	☐
4.	Kite	✓	☐
5.	Light it or burn it	✓	☐
6.	Bad breath	✓	☐
7.	The Pope	✓	☐

Mark: 'There's been lots of debate about who has the largest following on Twitter, but it's been claimed that if you add up the Pope's various official Twitter accounts – his tweets are available in at least six different languages – it's him. At the time of writing, at least.'

		THE BEAST	YOU
8.	Wallis	✓	☐

Mark: 'Wallis Simpson was the first woman to be named 'Person of the Year' by Time magazine.'

		THE BEAST	YOU
9.	Butterscotch	✗	☐
10.	Embrace	✗	☐
11.	*The Da Vinci Code*	✓	☐
12.	Edison Lighthouse	✗	☐
13.	Arthur Scargill	✓	☐
14.	Porsche	✓	☐

	THE BEAST	YOU
15. Crystal Palace	✓	☐
16. Macau	✓	☐
17. Garfield	✓	☐
18. Tuna	✓	☐
19. Victoria Principal	✓	☐
20. Sanskrit	✗	☐
21. Noddy	✓	☐
22. Lobster	✗	☐
23. Christian Bale (Batman actors)	✓	☐
24. Jupiter	✓	☐

> Mark: 'The reason the "Planets" suite only has seven movements is because Holst didn't include Earth, and Pluto hadn't been discovered yet.'

	THE BEAST	YOU
25. Rupert Murdoch	✗	☐
26. MSG (monosodium glutomate)	✗	☐
27. Scatterbrook Farm	✓	☐
28. Abortion	✓	☐
29. Ibrox	✓	☐
30. Young Disciples	✗	☐
SCORE	22/30	___/30

GENERAL KNOWLEDGE 5 – EASY

		THE BEAST	YOU
1.	Steven Spielberg	✓	☐
2.	Veganism	✓	☐
3.	Florida	✓	☐
4.	Jupiter	✓	☐
5.	Italy	✓	☐
6.	Transformers	✓	☐

> *Mark: 'A Holocaust survivor, toymaker and professional poker player, Henry Orenstein not only designed the Transformers, he also helped popularize the game of poker by inventing a camera set-up in the 1990s that allowed TV viewers to see the players' hole cards, making the game much more fun to watch.'*

		THE BEAST	YOU
7.	Michelangelo	✓	☐
8.	Lithium	✓	☐
9.	Norway	✓	☐
10.	Vodka	✓	☐
11.	Argentina	✓	☐
12.	Bats	✓	☐
13.	Edward I	✓	☐
14.	Genesis	✓	☐
15.	Fool's gold	✓	☐
16.	Adolf Hitler	✓	☐
17.	John le Carré	✓	☐

	THE BEAST	YOU
18. Horse	✓	☐
19. Namibia	✓	☐
20. Austria	✓	☐
21. Madrid	✓	☐
22. *Dombey and Son*	✗	☐
23. Samovar	✓	☐
24. Machine Gun Kelly	✗	☐
25. James Cameron	✓	☐

> **Mark: 'In 2010, James Cameron's ex-wife Kathryn Bigelow beat him to the Best Picture and Best Director Oscars with The Hurt Locker. *He had been nominated for* Avatar.'**

	THE BEAST	YOU
26. Curly (McLain)	✓	☐
27. Othello Syndrome	✓	☐
28. Devil's Island	✓	☐
29. *101 Dalmatians*	✓	☐
30. World's Strongest Man	✓	☐
SCORE	**28/30**	___/30

		THE BEAST	YOU
1.	Yellowstone	✓	☐
2.	Vincent van Gogh	✓	☐
3.	*The Sixth Sense*	✓	☐
4.	Vesuvius	✓	☐
5.	Graffiti	✓	☐
6.	Zirconium	✓	☐
7.	Lannister	✓	☐
8.	Down	✓	☐
9.	The Honky Tonk Man	✓	☐

Mark: 'Roy Wayne Farris is old-skool WWE. Born in Memphis, he says he never really wanted to adopt the Elvis look, but when a dedicated wrestling fan made him an Elvis-style jumpsuit to wear on his way to the ring, the look stuck.'

		THE BEAST	YOU
10.	Sombrero	✓	☐
11.	Bad Bunny	✗	☐
12.	Wendy Carlos	✗	☐
13.	Giraffe	✗	☐
14.	'Helter Skelter'	✗	☐
15.	Clarity	✓	☐
16.	Elizabeth Taylor	✓	☐
17.	Ras el hanout	✗	☐
18.	*Wicked*	✓	☐

	THE BEAST	YOU
19. Skirt	✓	☐
20. Escape velocity	✓	☐
21. Afghan girl	✓	☐
22. Great Fire of London	✓	☐

Mark: 'The year in question is 1666, which is MDCLXVI in Roman numerals.'

	THE BEAST	YOU
23. Ecclesiastes	✗	☐
24. Angel Falls	✓	☐
25. Urban Decay	✓	☐
26. (Green) cedar	✓	☐
27. Vonda Shepard	✗	☐
28. Uluru	✓	☐

Mark: 'Uluru is the world's largest single rock monolith. That is to say, there is no other single rock formation as large as Uluru. While Mount Augustus in Western Australia is much larger, it contains a variety of rock types.'

	THE BEAST	YOU
29. Kenneth Arrow	✗	☐
30. Meryl Streep	✗	☐
SCORE	21/30	___/30

GENERAL KNOWLEDGE 7 – MEDIUM

		THE BEAST	YOU
1.	Abraham Lincoln	✓	☐
2.	Tennessee Williams	✓	☐
3.	*Playboy*	✓	☐
4.	Lasagne	✗	☐
5.	Nelson Mandela	✓	☐
6.	Golden Girls	✓	☐

> Mark: 'When Estelle Getty got the role of Sophia, she was 62 – one year younger than Bea Arthur, who played her on-screen daughter, Dorothy. Betty White, who played Rose, outlived her co-stars and died on New Year's Eve 2021, just weeks before her 100th birthday.'

		THE BEAST	YOU
7.	HMS *Beagle*	✓	☐
8.	Heart	✓	☐
9.	Giraffe	✓	☐
10.	Simone de Beauvoir	✗	☐
11.	Hispaniola	✓	☐
12.	Viagra	✓	☐
13.	Tom Parker	✓	☐
14.	Steve Winwood	✓	☐
15.	Cesar Romero	✓	☐
16.	*Boogie Nights*	✓	☐
17.	Alice Walker	✓	☐

	THE BEAST	YOU
18. Max Factor	✓	☐
19. Ted Danson	✓	☐
20. The Doctor	✓	☐
21. Naomie Harris	✓	☐
22. El Salvador	✓	☐

> **Mark: 'This conflict is also known as the Football War. Here's my trick for remembering all the countries of Central America – "Great Britain Every Home Near Central Point". That gives you Guatemala, Belize, El Salvador, Honduras, Nicaragua, Costa Rica and Paraguay.'**

	THE BEAST	YOU
23. Whitney Houston	✗	☐
24. San Marino	✓	☐
25. Pituitary	✗	☐
26. Phoenix	✓	☐
27. Cuba	✓	☐
28. Endometriosis	✗	☐
29. Diane Warren	✗	☐
30. Spain	✓	☐
SCORE	**24/30**	__/30

GENERAL KNOWLEDGE 8 – MEDIUM

		THE BEAST	YOU
1.	Marilyn Monroe	✓	☐
2.	Diamond	✓	☐

> Mark: 'Diamonds have the highest refractive index of any naturally known substance. That's why they are so sparkly – light bends on entering a diamond and comes back out at all kinds of angles.'

3.	Giuseppe Verdi	✓	☐
4.	Perth	✓	☐
5.	Starbucks	✓	☐

> Mark: 'The coffee chain was originally going to be called either Cargo House or Pequod, after Captain Ahab's ship in Moby Dick – instead, it's named after a member of the ship's crew.'

6.	Mojito	✓	☐
7.	Carl Linnaeus	✓	☐
8.	Wario	✓	☐
9.	Bob the Builder	✓	☐
10.	Creedence Clearwater Revival	✓	☐
11.	Ned Flanders	✓	☐
12.	Brothers	✓	☐
13.	Brahma	✗	☐
14.	*Green Book*	✗	☐

	THE BEAST	YOU
15. Versailles	✓	☐
16. Christina	✓	☐
17. IMF	✓	☐
18. AC/DC	✓	☐
19. Santiago	✓	☐
20. Middleweight	✓	☐
21. *Network*	✓	☐

Mark: 'This line was said by Peter Finch in Network. He was the first actor to win a posthumous Oscar. He died of a heart attack at the age of 60, only a few months before the ceremony took place.'

	THE BEAST	YOU
22. Roubaix	✓	☐
23. Brunei	✗	☐
24. M	✓	☐
25. Pan's People	✓	☐
26. *Moana*	✓	☐
27. Volgograd	✗	☐
28. Boston Celtics	✓	☐
29. *The College Dropout*	✗	☐
30. Wilhelm Röntgen	✗	☐
SCORE	24/30	___/30

GENERAL KNOWLEDGE 9 – MEDIUM

		THE BEAST	YOU
1.	Doctor Who	✓	☐
2.	'Common People'	✓	☐
3.	Bin or trash can	✓	☐
4.	Cheese	✓	☐
5.	Ghost	✓	☐
6.	Panorama	✓	☐
7.	Sri Lanka	✓	☐
8.	Jimmy Hoffa	✓	☐
9.	Spanish	✓	☐
10.	Meg Ryan	✓	☐
11.	Indian ink	✗	☐
12.	Roy Hattersley	✓	☐
13.	Green and gold	✓	☐
14.	Victoria	✓	☐
15.	Lion	✓	☐
16.	Bloody Sunday	✓	☐
17.	Oldham	✗	☐
18.	Djibouti	✓	☐
19.	Faroe Islands	✓	☐

ANSWERS   243

	THE BEAST	YOU
20. *Songs of Praise*	✓	☐

> Mark: 'In the 1990s, when the show was still getting 6 million viewers, more people were watching Songs of Praise *than attending church in the UK each week.'*

	THE BEAST	YOU
21. The X-Factor	✓	☐
22. Wind of Change	✓	☐
23. Mercia	✓	☐
24. Bread	✗	☐
25. Blood	✓	☐
26. Humphrey Bogart	✗	☐
27. Idlewild	✓	☐
28. *Julius Caesar*	✓	☐
29. Dining or eating	✗	☐
30. Dominican Republic	✗	☐
SCORE	24/30	___/30

GENERAL KNOWLEDGE 10 – MEDIUM

		THE BEAST	YOU
1.	Two fat ladies	✓	☐
2.	Edinburgh	✓	☐
3.	Chicago	✓	☐
4.	Piano keys	✓	☐
5.	Snap	✓	☐
6.	South Park	✓	☐
7.	Gwen Stefani	✓	☐
8.	Jazeera	✓	☐
9.	Q(ueue)	✓	☐
10.	Hare	✓	☐
11.	Harrison Ford	✓	☐
12.	Javelin	✓	☐
13.	Genius	✓	☐
14.	Jerusalem	✓	☐
15.	Toledo	✓	☐
16.	Formosa	✓	☐
17.	High Noon	✓	☐
18.	Lion	✓	☐
19.	Nickel	✓	☐
20.	Irwell	✓	☐
21.	Yakult	✗	☐

	THE BEAST	YOU
22. Mark Cavendish	✓	☐

Mark: 'In 2021, Mark Cavendish equalled the long-standing Tour de France stage-win record, held by the five-times winner Eddy Merckx, with the 34th stage win of his career.'

	THE BEAST	YOU
23. 'Poison Ivy'	✗	☐
24. Farfalle	✓	☐
25. Nellie the Elephant	✓	☐

Mark: 'I set a counter question to this for a quiz once, asking which Toy Dolls hit mentions the name of a president more than 30 times in the lyrics. When Nellie says goodbye to the circus, she goes off "with a trumpety-trump, trump, trump, trump".'

	THE BEAST	YOU
26. Ursula	✓	☐
27. Peru	✓	☐
28. Seven	✓	☐
29. Oktoberfest	✓	☐
30. *Girls Next Door*	✓	☐
SCORE	**28/30**	__/30

GENERAL KNOWLEDGE 11 – TOUGH

		THE BEAST	YOU
1.	*Hair* (Not *Hairspray*)	✓	☐
2.	Intranet	✗	☐
3.	Marilyn Monroe	✓	☐
4.	Puerto Rico	✓	☐
5.	Sinistral	✓	☐

Mark: 'Ambidextrous people can use both hands like a right-handed person uses their right hand. In panto, the convention is for the villain to enter from the left of the stage and the hero from the right.'

		THE BEAST	YOU
6.	Yellow	✓	☐
7.	Technetium	✓	☐

Mark: 'In the early versions of the periodic table he formulated in the late 19th century, Mendeleev left a gap between elements 42 and 44 for an element that he thought should be there, but just hadn't been found yet. Technetium was finally discovered in 1937.'

		THE BEAST	YOU
8.	Obsidian	✓	☐

Mark: 'Stone Age people used obsidian weapons, and they were very sharp – just like the dragon glass weapons in Game of Thrones.'

		THE BEAST	YOU
9.	*Cholera*	✓	☐

	THE BEAST	YOU
10. Indiana Jones	✓	☐
11. 225 (also accept 220–230)	✗	☐
12. Kelsey Grammer	✓	☐

> *Mark: 'Kelsey Grammer earned Emmy nominations for playing Dr Frasier Crane in* Cheers *in 1988 and 1990. He was nominated in 1992 for a crossover appearance as Frasier on* Wings, *in an episode titled 'Planes, Trains, and Visiting Cranes'. He was also nominated for an Emmy award 10 times for his own series,* Frasier.'

13. Boudoir	✓	☐
14. GOAT (greatest of all time)	✗	☐
15. Horse bit	✗	☐
16. Wallace (and Gromit)	✗	☐
17. Pain	✓	☐
18. On tenterhooks	✗	☐
19. Sunny Delight	✓	☐
20. Dallas	✓	☐
21. The Loch Ness Monster	✗	☐
22. Eurovision Song Contest	✓	☐
23. Reykjavik	✗	☐
24. Peas (frozen)	✗	☐
25. 14th century	✓	☐
26. Committing suicide	✗	☐

	THE BEAST	YOU
27. John Cleese	✓	☐
28. Sheep	✗	☐
29. Manuka honey	✓	☐
30. Stratosphere	✗	☐
SCORE	**18/30**	**___/30**

GENERAL KNOWLEDGE 12 – TOUGH

	THE BEAST	YOU
1. *The Curse of the Black Pearl*	✓	☐
2. 'Maggie May' (Thatcher and Theresa)	✓	☐
3. Only had one hand	✓	☐
4. Brontë sisters	✓	☐
5. Desmond Morris	✓	☐
6. Quidditch	✓	☐
7. Katharine Hepburn	✗	☐
8. Nullarbor Plain	✓	☐

> **Mark: 'Some say the Nullarbor Plain is a desert, some say it's a plain. Either way, it's dry! Part of the world's longest fence, built to keep out dingoes, runs through it for hundreds of miles, as does the Trans-Australian Railway.'**

	THE BEAST	YOU
9. Bastet (also accept bast)	✓	☐
10. Pakistan	✗	☐
11. Crocodile	✓	☐
12. *Boris Godunov*	✓	☐
13. Save the Children	✓	☐
14. Peru	✗	☐
15. Tom Daley	✓	☐
16. Friday	✓	☐
17. Trilby	✗	☐
18. Larry Flynt	✓	☐

	THE BEAST	YOU
19. *The Spy Who Loved Me*	✓	☐
20. Only horse not to fall	✓	☐
21. Kardashian	✓	☐
22. Crash	✗	☐
23. Lilith	✓	☐
24. Sir Stamford Raffles	✓	☐

Mark: 'Sir Stamford Raffles was a collector and scholar who researched the natural and cultural history, civilization and languages of what is now Indonesia and Malaysia. His History of Java was published in 1817. As well as founding modern Singapore, he also founded London Zoo.'

	THE BEAST	YOU
25. Orion's Belt	✓	☐
26. Martin	✓	☐
27. Charles de Gaulle	✓	☐
28. Gander	✓	☐
29. Mississippi	✗	☐
30. *Eats, Shoots & Leaves*	✓	☐
SCORE	24/30	___/30

GENERAL KNOWLEDGE 13 – TOUGH

	THE BEAST	YOU
1. Mr. Tickle	✓	☐
2. Cooper	✓	☐
3. 17	✓	☐
4. Power	✓	☐

> **Mark:** *'One horsepower is equal to 746 watts. When an engine is said to be capable of 300 horsepower, that's how it's calculated.'*

	THE BEAST	YOU
5. Zelda	✓	☐

> **Mark:** *'The late Robin Williams named his daughter Zelda in honour of the game, because he played it so much.'*

	THE BEAST	YOU
6. Martello towers	✓	☐
7. Louisiana	✓	☐
8. Alice Cooper	✓	☐
9. Handcuffs	✗	☐
10. Carpathians	✗	☐
11. Lea & Perrins	✓	☐
12. Roadrunner	✓	☐
13. Davy Crockett	✓	☐
14. Ultimate Fighting/UFC (also accept MMA or Mixed Martial Arts)	✓	☐

Mark: 'In the beginning, there were hardly any rules in Ultimate Fighting, and no weight classes. To avoid their events being banned is some states of the US, the organizers started to introduce a series of regulations in the late 1990s.'

15. Richard II ✗ ☐

16. Red Army Faction (also accept Baader–Meinhof Gang) ✓ ☐

17. 'Allo 'Allo ✓ ☐

18. Banana ✗ ☐

19. Johnny Briggs (also played Mike Baldwin) ✗ ☐

20. Uncle Tom's Cabin ✓ ☐

21. NATO ✓ ☐

22. Bungee jumping ✓ ☐

23. Klingon ✓ ☐

24. Jonas Salk ✗ ☐

25. The Rodney King beating ✓ ☐

26. Daedalus ✓ ☐

27. The Prince and the Pauper ✓ ☐

28. Louis XIV (both name and number required) ✓ ☐

29. Seven (H, K, L, M, N, P, W) ✗ ☐

30. Soles ✗ ☐

SCORE 22/30 ___/30

GENERAL KNOWLEDGE 14 – TOUGH

		THE BEAST	YOU
1.	Felix	✗	☐
2.	Hill	✓	☐
3.	Andorra	✓	☐
4.	*The Witches of Eastwick*	✓	☐
5.	Isle of Man	✓	☐
6.	It's when Abraham Lincoln was shot (at Ford's Theatre)	✓	☐
7.	Llandudno	✓	☐
8.	Inspector Morse	✓	☐

Mark: 'There were 33 episodes of the Morse TV series, produced between 1987 and 2000. Since then, there have been more episodes of the prequel series Endeavour *(36 episodes) than there were of the original. There were also 33 episodes of the spin-off series* Lewis.'

		THE BEAST	YOU
9.	Liam Gallagher (his brother)	✓	☐
10.	New Zealand	✓	☐
11.	Chewbacca	✓	☐
12.	Jake Bugg	✗	☐
13.	Royal Mint	✓	☐

Mark: 'Before moving to Wales, the Royal Mint was based in the Tower of London.'

		THE BEAST	YOU
14.	Glen Campbell	✓	☐

	THE BEAST	YOU
15. Olive Oyl	✓	☐
16. Scarborough	✓	☐
17. Genesis	✓	☐
18. Sodor (home of Thomas the Tank Engine)	✗	☐
19. Harley-Davidson	✗	☐
20. *The Likely Lads*	✓	☐
21. Stour	✓	☐
22. They were both horses (Secretariat & Man o' War)	✗	☐
23. Mike Nesmith	✓	☐
24. 1545	✓	☐

Mark: 'To work this out, you have to know there's a treble, a double and two singles for each number from 1 to 20. I worked out that the numbers from 1 to 20 add up to 210, then multiplied that by 7 (because 3 + 2 + 1 + 1 = 7), which makes 1470. Then I added 25 for the outer bull and 50 for the inner bull. And I did this in under 10 seconds. ☺'

	THE BEAST	YOU
25. *Misery*	✗	☐
26. The flag had all 50 stars on – there were not 50 states at that time	✗	☐
27. All discovered by mistake	✗	☐
28. Ultraviolet	✓	☐

	THE BEAST	YOU
29. Antimony	✓	☐
30. Sperm whale	✓	☐
SCORE	22/30	___/30

		THE BEAST	YOU
1.	John Paul Young	✗	☐
2.	Yahoo!	✓	☐
3.	Woodstock	✓	☐
4.	Lisbon	✓	☐
5.	Ralph	✓	☐
6.	Horror	✓	☐

> **Mark: 'Before making zombie films, Romero got his start by directing short segments for the US kids' TV show Mr Rogers' Neighborhood.'**

7.	N	✓	☐
8.	Quentin Crisp	✓	☐
9.	Polynesia	✓	☐
10.	Ronald Reagan	✓	☐
11.	Modena	✗	☐
12.	Elijah Wood	✓	☐
13.	Vanuatu	✓	☐
14.	Turing Test	✓	☐
15.	*Spectre*	✓	☐
16.	Respect	✓	☐
17.	Scorpio	✗	☐
18.	Zulu	✗	☐
19.	*Tosca*	✗	☐

	THE BEAST	YOU
20. Domino	✗	☐
21. Paternoster	✓	☐
22. West-southwest	✓	☐
23. Ouagadougou	✓	☐
24. Shall I compare thee to a summer's day?	✓	☐
25. Scalp (also accept hair)	✓	☐
26. 'Happy Talk'	✓	☐
27. Erin Brockovich herself	✓	☐
28. Aussie rules football	✓	☐
29. Texas (NASA's Mission Control is in Houston)	✓	☐
30. 'A Touch of Class'	✓	☐

Mark: 'When the first series of Fawlty Towers aired in 1975, it got scathing reviews and low ratings. But when it was repeated, it began to gain an audience and is now considered a classic. There have been three American shows based on Fawlty Towers – Snavely (1978), which never made it past the pilot episode, Amanda's (1983), which starred Bea Arthur and was cancelled after ten episodes, and Payne, which ran for eight episodes in 1999.'

SCORE 24/30 ___/30

GENERAL KNOWLEDGE 16 – BRUTAL

		THE BEAST	YOU
1.	Linda Gray (Sue Ellen)	✓	☐
2.	Galapagos	✓	☐
3.	The Cenotaph	✓	☐
4.	Bolton Wanderers	✗	☐
5.	Tintoretto	✗	☐
6.	Arnold Bennett	✗	☐
7.	Terence Higgins Trust	✓	☐
8.	Masherbrum	✗	☐
9.	Edvard Grieg	✓	☐
10.	Chris Hoy	✓	☐
11.	Turkey	✗	☐
12.	Alcatraz	✓	☐
13.	Kodak	✗	☐
14.	Disco Duck	✗	☐
15.	Blackbeard	✓	☐
16.	Beamish	✓	☐
17.	Qashqai	✗	☐
18.	Sam Peckinpah	✓	☐
19.	Dreamcast	✗	☐
20.	Baseball (World Series)	✗	☐

	THE BEAST	YOU
21. Rio de Janeiro	✓	☐

> *Mark: 'The cruising altitude of Concorde was almost 60,000 feet, which is higher than the official ceiling for planes like the F-16. It's high enough to see the curvature of the Earth and the darkness of space.'*

	THE BEAST	YOU
22. Two	✓	☐
23. Finland	✓	☐
24. Jimmy Carter	✗	☐
25. Types of knot	✗	☐
26. *Cloudy with a Chance of Meatballs*	✓	☐
27. Pull out their hair	✗	☐
28. 56	✓	☐
29. A cohort	✓	☐
30. Moccasin	✓	☐
SCORE	17/30	___/30

GENERAL KNOWLEDGE 17 – BRUTAL

		THE BEAST	YOU
1.	*The Blues Brothers*	✓	☐
2.	Kylie Minogue	✓	☐
3.	Enoch	✗	☐
4.	France	✓	☐
5.	First Black officer in the Met	✗	☐
6.	*The Running Man*	✓	☐
7.	Fort Sumter	✓	☐
8.	Tangerine Dream	✗	☐
9.	Diaspora	✓	☐
10.	Dr Magnus Pyke	✓	☐
11.	Bentley	✓	☐
12.	Wychwood	✗	☐
13.	Mary Seacole	✓	☐
14.	Ludo	✗	☐
15.	Waikato	✗	☐
16.	Piano	✗	☐
17.	Potsdam	✗	☐
18.	Scoliosis (curved spine)	✓	☐
19.	General Zod	✓	☐
20.	Engelbert Humperdinck	✓	☐
21.	15	✓	☐
22.	Ethiopia	✗	☐
23.	Owl	✓	☐

	THE BEAST	YOU
24. Designed the old and new World Trade Center	✓	☐
25. Chipolata	✗	☐
26. Margot Kidder	✓	☐
27. Oliver Twist	✓	☐
28. Mezzaluna	✓	☐
29. Banana republic	✓	☐
30. Ezra Pound	✗	☐
SCORE	**19/30**	**___/30**

		THE BEAST	YOU
1.	*Only Connect*	✓	☐
2.	Harold	✓	☐
3.	California Gold Rush	✓	☐
4.	Calgary (1988)	✓	☐

> Mark: *'Due to his being extremely long-sighted, Eddie was forced to wear eyeglasses at all times. They would fog up beneath his ski goggles, rendering him nearly blind during his jumps.'*

		THE BEAST	YOU
5.	The Epsom Derby	✓	☐
6.	Paul VI	✗	☐
7.	Dingwall	✗	☐
8.	Egypt	✓	☐
9.	Watney's Red Barrel	✗	☐
10.	Gucci	✗	☐
11.	USS *Phoenix* (later renamed *The General Belgrano*)	✓	☐
12.	A type of cannon	✓	☐
13.	Kenneth Williams	✓	☐
14.	*Saved by the Bell*	✓	☐
15.	Holly Johnson	✓	☐
16.	Jack Vettriano	✓	☐
17.	Nathan's	✗	☐
18.	Doc Cox	✗	☐

	THE BEAST	YOU
19. (Old) Tom Parr	✗	☐
20. Larch	✗	☐
21. Propaganda	✓	☐
22. Lyon	✓	☐
23. Mount Gay	✗	☐
24. Van Pelt	✗	☐
25. 36	✓	☐
26. The Cairngorms	✓	☐
27. Wallis Simpson	✗	☐
28. Murder Incorporated	✓	☐
29. Groucho Marx	✗	☐
30. *Octopussy*	✓	☐
SCORE	18/30	___/30

GENERAL KNOWLEDGE 19 – BRUTAL

		THE BEAST	YOU
1.	Uranus	✓	☐
2.	Reform Club	✓	☐
3.	Iguazu Falls	✓	☐

> Mark: 'Iguazu Falls, which means "big water", consists of 275 different waterfalls. The falls are taller and wider than Niagara Falls and were used as a backdrop in films including Moonraker, Miami Vice and Black Panther.'

		THE BEAST	YOU
4.	Train times or information	✓	☐
5.	Mead	✓	☐
6.	Colonel Gadaffi	✗	☐
7.	Isla Nublar	✓	☐
8.	Lebanon	✗	☐
9.	Quintain	✓	☐
10.	Erebus	✓	☐
11.	Go	✓	☐
12.	James Earl Jones	✓	☐
13.	Ugly Sisters	✓	☐
14.	Hawkeye	✓	☐
15.	Frigga	✓	☐
16.	Orangutan	✓	☐
17.	Ludwig Ritter von Köchel	✓	☐
18.	Rapunzel	✓	☐

	THE BEAST	YOU
19. The Qu'ran	✓	☐
20. Upsilon	✗	☐
21. David Beckham	✓	☐
22. Tommy Lee Jones	✓	☐
23. Lupo	✗	☐
24. 1 kilometre to go	✓	☐
25. Wyoming	✗	☐
26. Violet Beauregarde	✓	☐
27. New Orleans (Big Apple to Big Easy)	✗	☐
28. Brain freeze or ice-cream headache	✗	☐
29. Mexico	✓	☐
30. Tracey Ullman	✓	☐

Mark: 'Tracey Ullman is best known as a comedian and actress, but she is also a screenwriter, director, producer, author, businesswoman, dancer and singer. Originally from Britain, she holds American citizenship. She is best friends with Meryl Streep and has been nominated for 24 Emmys.'

SCORE 23/30 ___/30

GENERAL KNOWLEDGE 20 – BRUTAL

		THE BEAST	YOU
1.	Harold Holt	✓	☐
2.	Josiah Bartlett/Bartlet	✓	☐
3.	Little Bighorn	✓	☐
4.	Primeval	✓	☐
5.	Earl Grey	✓	☐
6.	Ted Moult	✓	☐
7.	Coccyx	✗	☐
8.	LBW	✓	☐
9.	Pentecost	✓	☐
10.	Lisbon	✗	☐
11.	Memsahib	✓	☐
12.	Draughts	✗	☐
13.	1910	✓	☐
14.	Moist von Lipwig	✓	☐
15.	Gamay	✗	☐

Mark: 'Within the Beaujolais region, which is 34 miles long from north to south and 7 to 9 miles wide, nearly 4,000 growers pick their Gamay grapes by hand in order to qualify for the Beaujolais Nouveau AOC. With the exception of Champagne, Beaujolais is the only wine to require this manner of grape collection.'

16.	Chaebols	✗	☐
17.	Kalends	✓	☐

	THE BEAST	YOU
18. Urticaria	✓	☐
19. William Daniels	✗	☐
20. Anchor	✗	☐
21. Pork pie	✓	☐
22. Chad	✓	☐
23. Women's 800m	✓	☐
24. Bob Marley	✓	☐
25. His own	✓	☐
26. *Angel Delight*	✓	☐
27. Pig	✓	☐
28. Jessica Fletcher	✗	☐

Mark: 'In its twelfth and final season, Murder She Wrote was moved to Thursday evenings in the US, up against Friends and Mad About You. Angela Lansbury, who played mystery writer Jessica Fletcher, expressed her sadness at the show being moved from its usual Sunday timeslot. In one episode titled 'Murder Among Friends', a TV producer is killed after planning to get rid of a member of the cast of a fictional television show called Buds – a thinly veiled pop at Friends.'

	THE BEAST	YOU
29. Dorian Gray	✓	☐
30. Lady's	✗	☐
SCORE	21/30	___/30

THE 1960s

		THE BEAST	YOU
1.	Yuri Gagarin	✓	☐

> *Mark: 'This happened on 12 April 1961 – 100 years to the day after the start of the American Civil War.'*

2.	Alcatraz	✓	☐
3.	René Magritte	✓	☐
4.	'These Boots Are Made for Walkin''	✓	☐
5.	Albert Camus	✓	☐

> *Mark: 'There's a thing about goalkeepers: Albert Camus played in goal for Algeria, Pope John Paul II was a good amateur goalie and, of course, Spanish crooner Julio Iglesias played for Real Madrid's second team.'*

6.	Linus Pauling	✓	☐
7.	Caernarvon	✓	☐
8.	Ronald Reagan	✓	☐
9.	Katanga	✗	☐
10.	*Mary Poppins*	✓	☐
11.	Tet Offensive	✓	☐
12.	Golda Meir	✓	☐
13.	Cassius Clay	✓	☐
14.	Torrey Canyon	✓	☐
15.	Sophia Loren	✓	☐

	THE BEAST	YOU
16. Martin Luther King Jr	✓	☐

'Mark: At the age of 35, Martin Luther King Jr was the youngest-ever winner of the Nobel Peace Prize. In 2014, Malala Yousafzai was awarded the prize at the incredible age of 14!'

17. Edward 'Ed' White	✗	☐
18. Italy	✗	☐
19. Richard Nixon	✓	☐

Mark: 'Nixon's the only person to have twice won the presidential AND vice-presidential elections.'

20. Bert Bacharach and Hal David	✗	☐
21. Paul VI	✓	☐
22. Olduvai Gorge	✓	☐
23. Yves Saint Laurent	✓	☐
24. *In Cold Blood*	✗	☐
25. Africa	✓	☐
26. *Last Exit to Brooklyn*	✓	☐
27. Blenheim Palace	✓	☐
28. Tokyo	✓	☐
29. Marie Goeppert-Mayer	✗	☐
30. Beatles	✓	☐
SCORE	24/30	___/30

THE 1970s

		THE BEAST	YOU
1.	Margaret Thatcher	✓	☐
2.	Elvis Presley	✓	☐

> *Mark: 'The Robin Hood pub in Cardiff, where I used to drink, had a framed ticket on the wall that the landlord had bought for an Elvis concert that was due to take place about a month after the singer died in 1977.'*

		THE BEAST	YOU
3.	Comic-Con	✓	☐
4.	Magic 8 Ball	✓	☐
5.	Richard Nixon	✓	☐
6.	The Post-it Note	✓	☐
7.	Jaws	✓	☐
8.	Chile	✓	☐
9.	Jon Pertwee	✓	☐
10.	Email	✓	☐
11.	Ceefax	✓	☐
12.	Munich, West Germany (1972)	✓	☐
13.	Atari	✓	☐
14.	The Terracotta Army	✓	☐
15.	Kermit the Frog	✓	☐
16.	'Bridge Over Troubled Water'	✓	☐
17.	Judy Blume	✗	☐

	THE BEAST	YOU
18. Miss World	✓	☐

> *Mark: 'She was Miss Puerto Rico.'*

	THE BEAST	YOU
19. 'Bohemian Rhapsody'	✓	☐
20. Antony Armstrong-Jones (later Lord Snowdon)	✓	☐
21. The Chopper	✓	☐
22. Made it legal to vote at 18 (previously 21)	✗	☐
23. Today is Saturday, watch and smile	✗	☐
24. The Netherlands	✓	☐
25. Farrokh Bulsara	✓	☐
26. Cyclone Tracy	✓	☐
27. Mother Teresa	✓	☐
28. The Wombles	✓	☐
29. My Chemical Romance	✗	☐
30. Lon Nol	✗	☐
SCORE	25/30	___/30

THE 1980s

		THE BEAST	YOU
1.	Sally Ride	✓	☐
2.	Netherlands (also accept Holland)	✓	☐

> *Mark: 'The Netherlands is unusual in that it's had three successive Queens as head of state, until Queen Beatrix abdicated in 2013 and left the crown to her son, the incumbent King Willem-Alexander.'*

		THE BEAST	YOU
3.	Martin Luther King Jr	✓	☐
4.	*Exxon Valdez*	✓	☐
5.	Laura Davies	✓	☐
6.	*Reader's Digest*	✗	☐
7.	Dingo	✓	☐
8.	*Rainbow Warrior*	✓	☐
9.	Marvin Gaye	✓	☐
10.	Baby Doc	✓	☐
11.	Mark Thatcher	✓	☐
12.	Imre Nagy	✓	☐
13.	Turin Shroud or Holy Shroud	✓	☐

> *Mark: 'Carbon dating placed the shroud in either the 13th or 14th century, which rather scuppered the idea that it was Jesus' burial shroud.'*

		THE BEAST	YOU
14.	15	✓	☐
15.	Bolivia	✗	☐

	THE BEAST	YOU
16. Bing Crosby (daughter Mary)	✓	☐
17. *Vincennes*	✗	☐
18. Rupert Murdoch	✓	☐
19. Count	✓	☐
20. Pakistan	✓	☐
21. Mount St Helens	✓	☐
22. Mikhail Gorbachev	✗	☐
23. Gabriel García Márquez	✓	☐
24. Trevor Berbick	✓	☐

Mark: 'In 1981, Berbick was the last boxer to ever fight Muhammad Ali, so his defeat to Tyson kind of heralded a new heavyweight generation.'

	THE BEAST	YOU
25. Golden Temple (also accept Harmandir Sahib)	✓	☐
26. Smokey Robinson	✓	☐
27. Seoul	✓	☐
28. *Gandhi*	✓	☐
29. Oliver North (Irangate)	✓	☐
30. St Paul's Cathedral	✓	☐
SCORE	**26/30**	**___/30**

THE 1990s

	THE BEAST	YOU
1. Genetically modified	✓	☐
2. Elizabeth Taylor	✗	☐
3. PlayStation	✓	☐
4. Katrina and the Waves	✓	☐
5. Smoking	✓	☐
6. *Atlantis*	✓	☐
7. Tamagotchi	✓	☐

Mark: 'I remember some of my pupils got really upset when their Tamagotchi died!'

	THE BEAST	YOU
8. Tim Berners-Lee	✓	☐
9. Czechoslovakia	✓	☐
10. Nigeria	✓	☐
11. Auckland	✓	☐
12. Donald Trump	✗	☐
13. Stefan Dennis	✓	☐
14. Deep Blue	✓	☐

Mark: 'And nowadays, computers can use robotic arms to move real chess pieces around the board. In 2022, a chess computer broke the finger of a seven-year-old boy when the child moved too fast and confused the robot, who mistook his finger for a chess piece!'

	THE BEAST	YOU
15. Toyota	✓	☐
16. Maastricht Treaty	✓	☐
17. Mötley Crüe	✓	☐
18. Subway	✓	☐
19. *Gladiator*	✓	☐
20. *The Nightmare Before Christmas*	✓	☐
21. NAFTA	✓	☐
22. Heathrow	✓	☐
23. Vincent van Gogh	✓	☐
24. Yugoslavia	✗	☐
25. Pan Am	✓	☐
26. Georgia	✗	☐
27. The Queen Mother	✓	☐
28. BMW	✓	☐
29. Sri Lanka	✗	☐
30. Homosexuality	✓	☐
SCORE	25/30	___/30

THE 2000s

		THE BEAST	YOU
1.	India	✓	☐

> *Mark: 'The UN estimates that in 2023, India will overtake China to become the world's most populous nation.'*

		THE BEAST	YOU
2.	Wikipedia	✓	☐
3.	Salt Lake City	✓	☐
4.	The Bull Ring	✓	☐
5.	A380	✓	☐
6.	International Space Station	✓	☐
7.	Millie Bobby Brown	✓	☐
8.	Zoo	✓	☐
9.	iPhone	✓	☐
10.	Saddam Hussein	✗	☐
11.	Viscount Severn	✓	☐
12.	Malta and Cyprus	✓	☐
13.	HMP Maze (also called Long Kesh)	✓	☐
14.	'Fiery' Fred Trueman	✓	☐

> *Mark: 'Fred Trueman's daughter used to be married to Raquel Welch's son.'*

		THE BEAST	YOU
15.	Sweden	✓	☐
16.	Billie Eilish	✓	☐

	THE BEAST	YOU
17. Charles Ingram	✓	☐
18. Michael Schumacher	✓	☐
19. Spike Milligan	✓	☐
20. Benazir Bhutto	✓	☐

> Mark: 'When they were both students at Oxford, Benazir Bhutto introduced former British Prime Minister Theresa May to the man who would become her husband.'

	THE BEAST	YOU
21. Switzerland	✓	☐
22. *Pioneer 10*	✗	☐
23. Harvard	✓	☐
24. Chelsea	✓	☐
25. The Bird's Nest	✓	☐
26. 15	✗	☐
27. South Korea and Japan	✓	☐
28. *Minecraft*	✓	☐
29. Slavery	✓	☐
30. Homeland Security	✓	☐
SCORE	**27/30**	__/30

ANIMALS

		THE BEAST	YOU
1.	Komodo dragon	✓	☐
2.	Wandering albatross	✓	☐
3.	Narwhal	✓	☐
4.	Bamboo	✓	☐

> **Mark:** 'The daft part is that pandas are mildly allergic to bamboo, of all things. Giant pandas are a type of bear, and they still have a meat-eater's digestive system. But they have accidentally become increasingly specialized on one type of food, which they can't even digest efficiently, simply because it's easily available in their natural habitat.'

		THE BEAST	YOU
5.	(Plains) zebra	✓	☐
6.	Beluga	✓	☐
7.	Swifts	✓	☐
8.	(Honey) bees	✓	☐
9.	Ichthyology	✓	☐
10.	Dewclaw	✗	☐
11.	Goldeneye	✓	☐
12.	Stick insects	✓	☐
13.	Mauritius	✓	☐
14.	Secretary bird	✓	☐
15.	Salamanders	✓	☐
16.	Gastropoda or gastropods	✓	☐

	THE BEAST	YOU
17. Baleen	✓	☐

Mark: *'Baleen whales eat a diet largely consisting of krill, along with plankton and other tiny marine organisms. Some of the largest life forms on Earth feed on the very smallest.'*

	THE BEAST	YOU
18. Ounce	✓	☐
19. Goliath frog	✓	☐
20. Tortoise or turtle	✓	☐
21. Passerine	✗	☐
22. Chordata	✓	☐
23. Chrysalis	✓	☐
24. Kiwi	✓	☐
25. Gizzard	✓	☐
26. Aye-aye	✓	☐
27. Fruit flies	✓	☐
28. Coprolites or coproliths	✓	☐
29. Koala	✗	☐
30. Capuchin monkey	✓	☐
SCORE	27/30	___/30

ANSWER SMASH!

	THE BEAST	YOU
1. Michael Douglas Adams	✓	☐
2. Bruce Wayne Gretsky	✓	☐

> *Mark: 'Wayne Gretsky was house- and babysitting for his friend Alan Thicke in LA when he found out that he was being traded from the Edmonton Oilers to the Los Angeles Kings. Alan's son Robin Thicke, who was 11 at the time, went on to have a smash hit with "Blurred Lines".'*

	THE BEAST	YOU
3. Natalie Wood pigeon	✗	☐
4. Ray Charles Dickens	✓	☐
5. Watership Down to Earth	✓	☐
6. Stephen King Kong	✓	☐
7. Inspector (or Endeavour) Morse code	✓	☐
8. Basil Brush strokes	✓	☐
9. Jolly Roger Moore	✓	☐
10. Howard Donald Trump	✓	☐
11. Edward Fox hunting	✓	☐
12. Alan Partridge Family	✓	☐
13. John Terry Wogan	✓	☐
14. Goodluck Jonathan Creek	✗	☐
15. Mother T(h)eresa May	✗	☐
16. Roy Castle Howard	✓	☐
17. Fort William Hill	✓	☐

	THE BEAST	YOU
18. Open Sesame Street	✓	☐
19. Tiller Girls Aloud	✗	☐
20. Sahara Desert Orchid	✓	☐
21. Barbara Windsor Castle	✓	☐
22. Tammy Abraham Lincoln	✓	☐
23. Dawn French fries	✓	☐
24. Frank Bruno Tonioli	✓	☐
25. Herr Flick knife	✓	☐
26. Question Mark Spitz	✓	☐
27. Francis de la Tour de France	✓	☐
28. Michael Winner Takes It All	✓	☐
29. Da Doo Ron Ron Burgundy	✗	☐
30. 147 Break a leg	✓	☐
SCORE	**25/30**	**___/30**

ART

	THE BEAST	YOU
1. Marilyn Monroe	✓	☐
2. *Mona Lisa*	✓	☐

> Mark: 'It has been suggested that the picture might actually be a self-portrait, after artist Lillian Schwartz did a digital analysis that found similarities between the facial features of the Mona Lisa and Leonardo da Vinci's Portrait of a Man in Red Chalk, which is thought to be a self-portrait. Most experts disagree, though.'

	THE BEAST	YOU
3. Moulin Rouge	✓	☐
4. Clocks or watches	✓	☐
5. Seashell or scallop shell	✓	☐
6. *Whistler's Mother*	✓	☐
7. Triptych	✓	☐
8. Pointillism	✓	☐
9. Claude Monet	✓	☐
10. Diego Velázquez	✗	☐
11. *American Gothic*	✓	☐

> Mark: 'I believe the models for this painting were the artist's sister, Nan Wood Graham, and his dentist, Dr Byron McKeeby.'

	THE BEAST	YOU
12. (French) flag	✗	☐
13. Fresco	✗	☐

	THE BEAST	YOU
14. Photography	✗	☐
15. El Greco	✓	☐
16. New York	✓	☐
17. Ned Kelly	✓	☐
18. Apple	✓	☐
19. Green	✗	☐
20. Madame Tussaud	✓	☐

Mark: *'Madame Tussaud was imprisoned for three months during the French Revolution and even faced the guillotine, because she had been a regular visitor at Versailles, where she taught Madame Elizabeth, the sister of King Louis XVI of France, art.'*

	THE BEAST	YOU
21. Chiaroscuro	✗	☐
22. (Spider) monkeys	✗	☐
23. Antonio Canova	✗	☐
24. Trompe l'œil	✗	☐
25. Ansel Adams	✗	☐
26. Der Blaue Reiter or The Blue Rider	✓	☐
27. Hudson River	✓	☐
28. Berthe Morisot	✗	☐
29. Donatello	✓	☐
30. Lion	✗	☐
SCORE	18/30	___/30

BIOLOGY

		THE BEAST	YOU
1.	Carbon dioxide	✓	☐
2.	Achilles tendon	✓	☐
3.	Pollen	✓	☐
4.	Pandemic	✓	☐
5.	RNA (ribonucleic acid)	✓	☐
6.	Patella	✓	☐

> *Mark: 'Elephants are the only four-legged mammals with four knees – all the others have one pair of joints that face backwards, like elbows.'*

		THE BEAST	YOU
7.	Smallpox	✓	☐
8.	Vitamin C	✓	☐
9.	B	✓	☐
10.	Carboniferous	✓	☐

> *Mark: 'All the world's fossil fuels date back to the Carboniferous period. The fossilized remains of plants and animals were gradually converted into coal and oil over millions of years.'*

		THE BEAST	YOU
11.	Amniotic fluid	✓	☐
12.	Stoma	✗	☐
13.	Blood pressure	✓	☐

	THE BEAST	YOU
14. Syphilis	✓	☐

Mark: 'In the middle ages, the French called syphilis the English Pox, and the English called it the French Pox.'

15. Ketamine	✓	☐
16. Eye	✗	☐
17. Foot	✓	☐
18. Ecology	✓	☐
19. Parasympathetic	✗	☐
20. Rose	✓	☐
21. Chitin	✓	☐
22. Ethylene or ethene	✓	☐
23. Zika virus	✓	☐
24. Acetylcholine	✗	☐
25. Barr body	✓	☐
26. Dik-dik	✓	☐
27. Geranium	✗	☐
28. Barbara McClintock	✗	☐
29. Flagellum or flagella	✓	☐
30. Huntington's disease	✓	☐
SCORE	**24/30**	**___/30**

CHEMISTRY

	THE BEAST	YOU
1. Carbon	✓	☐
2. Hydrogen	✓	☐

> Mark: 'There's talk that what really caused the disaster was the material the Hindenburg was coated in, which was effectively a solid version of rocket fuel. Once that caught fire, it was far more explosive than hydrogen.'

3. DNA	✓	☐

> Mark: 'The missing figure in the discovery of DNA was Rosalind Franklin, who never got the credit she deserved. Franklin died at the age of 37 in 1958, and never learned the extent to which Watson and Crick had relied on her data to make their model.'

4. Sulphuric acid	✓	☐
5. Methane	✓	☐
6. Lead	✓	☐
7. Argon	✓	☐
8. Amino acids	✓	☐
9. Carbon monoxide or CO	✓	☐
10. Cholesterol	✓	☐
11. Aspirin (also accept acetylsalicylic acid)	✓	☐

> Mark: 'Aspirin was among the very first properly researched and developed pharmaceuticals.'

	THE BEAST	YOU
12. Magnesium	✗	☐
13. Lithium	✓	☐
14. Titanium	✓	☐
15. Doping	✗	☐
16. Rosalind Franklin	✓	☐
17. Palladium	✓	☐
18. Catalytic cracking	✓	☐
19. Antoine Lavoisier	✓	☐
20. Nitric acid (do not accept nitrous)	✓	☐
21. Cobalt	✗	☐
22. Osmium	✓	☐
23. Francium	✗	☐
24. (Radio) carbon dating	✓	☐
25. Introns	✗	☐
26. Ribosome	✗	☐
27. Uracil	✓	☐
28. Telomeres	✗	☐
29. Svante Arrhenius	✗	☐
30. CRISPR	✓	☐
SCORE	22/30	___/30

COMPUTER GAMES

		THE BEAST	YOU
1.	Nintendo	✓	☐
2.	*Fortnite*	✗	☐
3.	*Pac-Man*	✓	☐
4.	*FIFA*	✓	☐
5.	*Snake*	✓	☐
6.	Cortana	✗	☐
7.	Mario	✓	☐
8.	*Rocket League*	✓	☐
9.	*The Witcher*	✓	☐
10.	*Candy Crush*	✓	☐
11.	Monkey Island	✓	☐

> **Mark: 'In this game, you duel by using cunning quips!'**

		THE BEAST	YOU
12.	*Street Fighter*	✗	☐
13.	Rockstar Games	✓	☐
14.	*LEGO*	✓	☐
15.	Crash Bandicoot	✓	☐
16.	*The Sims*	✓	☐
17.	*Metroid*	✗	☐
18.	San Andreas	✓	☐

	THE BEAST	YOU
19. *Beat Saber*	✓	☐

> **Mark: 'It's actually a really good workout!'**

	THE BEAST	YOU
20. *Counter-Strike*	✓	☐
21. *RuneScape*	✓	☐
22. Bullet Bill	✗	☐
23. Platinum trophy	✓	☐
24. *Fall Guys*	✗	☐
25. *Five Nights at Freddy's*	✗	☐
26. Castle Crashers	✗	☐
27. *Hearthstone*	✗	☐
28. Rayman	✗	☐
29. Guitar (hero)	✓	☐
30. Ninja	✓	☐
SCORE	20/30	___/30

FASHION

		THE BEAST	YOU
1.	Christian Dior	✓	☐
2.	René Lacoste	✓	☐
3.	Kim Kardashian	✓	☐
4.	Vivienne Westwood	✓	☐
5.	Victoria Beckham	✓	☐
6.	Birkenstock	✗	☐
7.	Karl Lagerfeld	✓	☐
8.	Alexander McQueen	✗	☐
9.	Kappa Sports	✓	☐
10.	H&M	✓	☐
11.	Helly Hansen	✗	☐
12.	Ralph Lauren	✓	☐
13.	Gianni Versace	✓	☐

Mark: 'Gianni Versace was shot dead by Andrew Cunanan on the steps of his Miami house in 1997. Cunanan's motive is unknown, as he took his own life eight days later, on the run from the police.'

		THE BEAST	YOU
14.	Speedo	✓	☐
15.	Edward Enninful	✗	☐
16.	Stella Tennant	✗	☐

	THE BEAST	YOU
17. Harry Styles	✓	☐

> *Mark: 'On the cover of Vogue, Harry wore a voluminous pale blue gown paired with a black tuxedo jacket, both designed by Gucci.'*

	THE BEAST	YOU
18. Uniqlo	✗	☐
19. Balenciaga	✗	☐
20. Abercrombie & Fitch	✓	☐
21. Carolina Herrera	✗	☐
22. Zara	✓	☐
23. Karlie Kloss	✗	☐
24. David Gandy	✓	☐
25. Helena Rubinstein	✗	☐
26. Sergio Tacchini	✗	☐
27. Pretty Polly	✓	☐
28. Iris Apfel	✗	☐
29. Penhaligon's	✗	☐
30. Pat McGrath	✗	☐
SCORE	**16/30**	**___/30**

FILM

	THE BEAST	YOU
1. Shark (great white)	✓	☐

> *Mark: 'Peter Benchley, who wrote the novel that Jaws was based on, had a cameo role in the film and donated his fee to a charity.'*

	THE BEAST	YOU
2. Bruce Willis	✓	☐
3. The Avengers	✓	☐
4. Tom Hanks	✓	☐

> *Mark: 'Tom Hanks was the first actor to win Oscars in successive years (1993 and 1994) since Spencer Tracy won for Captains Courageous in 1937 and for Boys Town in 1938.'*

	THE BEAST	YOU
5. *Mary Poppins*	✓	☐
6. Dopey	✓	☐
7. '(I've Had) the Time of My Life'	✓	☐
8. Emma Watson	✓	☐
9. Vietnam War	✓	☐
10. *Top Gun*	✓	☐
11. Scottish	✓	☐
12. 88 mph	✓	☐
13. Drew Barrymore	✓	☐
14. Mathematics	✓	☐
15. Catwoman (Selina Kyle)	✓	☐

	THE BEAST	YOU
16. Bobsleigh	✓	☐
17. Basilisk	✓	☐
18. Chewbacca	✓	☐
19. *Uncharted*	✗	☐
20. The Holy Grail	✓	☐
21. Chimpanzee	✓	☐
22. The Great Train Robbery	✓	☐
23. *The African Queen*	✓	☐
24. Christmas Day	✓	☐
25. *The Shining*	✓	☐
26. *The Terminator*	✓	☐
27. Jaws	✓	☐
28. *The Sting*	✓	☐
29. Quentin Tarantino	✓	☐
30. East Great Falls High	✓	☐
SCORE	29/30	___/30

FOOD AND DRINK

		THE BEAST	YOU
1.	Rum	✓	☐
2.	Hawaii	✓	☐
3.	Tennessee	✗	☐
4.	Cadbury's	✓	☐
5.	Cosmopolitan	✓	☐
6.	Saffron	✓	☐
7.	Tequila	✓	☐

> **Mark:** 'George has made a fortune from tequila – not quite as much as he has from his acting career, but pretty close. George Foreman made more money from his "lean mean grilling machine" than he did from boxing.'

8.	Lemon	✓	☐
9.	Nigella Lawson	✓	☐
10.	Lamb	✓	☐
11.	Spinach	✓	☐
12.	White Russian	✗	☐
13.	Paprika	✓	☐
14.	Squid	✓	☐
15.	Japan	✓	☐
16.	Heston Blumenthal	✓	☐
17.	Viennetta	✓	☐
18.	Pizza Express	✓	☐

	THE BEAST	YOU
19. Spain	✓	☐
20. Grey Goose	✓	☐
21. Wendy's	✓	☐
22. Jamaica	✓	☐
23. Jollof	✓	☐
24. McDonald's	✓	☐
25. Dr Pepper	✓	☐
26. Hawksmoor	✗	☐
27. Darjeeling	✗	☐
28. Anthony Bourdain	✗	☐
29. Seagram	✗	☐
30. Copper	✓	☐

Mark: 'Copper is a good conductor of temperature, which helps keep the mule cold and frosty while also enhancing the vodka flavour and natural properties of the drink.'

SCORE   **24/30** ___/30

GEOGRAPHY 2

		THE BEAST	YOU
1.	Canada	✓	☐
2.	Volcanoes	✓	☐
3.	Mexico City	✓	☐
4.	Pacific	✓	☐
5.	Iraq	✓	☐
6.	Denmark	✓	☐
7.	Glacier	✓	☐
8.	Colorado River	✓	☐
9.	Animals	✓	☐
10.	Richter	✓	☐

Mark: 'There's also the Modified Mercalli Intensity Scale, which measures the observable effects of an earthquake, from weak tremors that only a few people will feel to buildings being destroyed.'

		THE BEAST	YOU
11.	Six	✗	☐
12.	Igneous rocks	✓	☐
13.	11	✓	☐

Mark: 'Russia has the most time zones of any country in the world. I learned that when I was eight years old, reading the Guinness Book of Records, and it's stayed in my brain.'

		THE BEAST	YOU
14.	Cape of Good Hope	✓	☐

	THE BEAST	YOU
15. David Attenborough	✓	☐
16. Left	✓	☐
17. An oxbow lake	✓	☐
18. South Dakota	✓	☐
19. Goulash	✓	☐
20. Stevenage	✓	☐
21. Baffin Island	✗	☐
22. Seattle	✓	☐
23. Zaire (now the Democratic Republic of the Congo)	✗	☐
24. Tunisia, Algeria and Morocco	✓	☐
25. Zambezi River	✓	☐
26. Namibia	✗	☐
27. Baku, Azerbaijan	✓	☐
28. Ten million+	✓	☐
29. Catatumbo	✗	☐
30. Nephology	✓	☐
SCORE	**25/30**	**___/30**

HISTORY PRE-1900

		THE BEAST	YOU
1.	The Lionheart	✓	☐
2.	Pirates	✓	☐

> *Mark: 'Anne Bonny was a young Irish woman who divorced her husband and married Calico Jack Rackham, a pirate captain, at sea. They teamed up with Mary Read and spent years living as pirates in the seas around Jamaica. In 1720, all three were captured and sentenced to death, along with the rest of Rackham's crew. Rackham was hanged and Mary died in prison, but there's no record of what happened to Anne.'*

3.	Salem	✓	☐
4.	Black Death or Bubonic Plague	✓	☐
5.	Republican	✓	☐
6.	Hundred Years War	✓	☐
7.	The Ides of March	✓	☐
8.	Louis XVI	✓	☐
9.	Spain	✓	☐
10.	White	✓	☐
11.	US Declaration of Independence	✓	☐
12.	Edward the Confessor	✓	☐
13.	Peeping Tom	✓	☐
14.	His horse	✓	☐
15.	Anne of Cleves	✓	☐

	THE BEAST	YOU
16. Mullet	✓	☐
17. Socrates	✓	☐
18. Jack the Ripper	✓	☐

> Mark: 'The five known victims of Jack the Ripper are Mary Ann Nichols, Annie Chapman, Elizabeth Stride, Catherine Eddowes and Mary Jane Kelly, but a 2019 BBC documentary suggested that a sixth woman, Martha Tabram, was an early victim.'

	THE BEAST	YOU
19. Aaron Burr	✗	☐
20. Appian Way	✓	☐
21. Chinese	✓	☐
22. Praetorian Guard	✓	☐
23. Ronin	✓	☐
24. The Mausoleum at Halicarnassus	✗	☐
25. Knossos	✓	☐
26. Hanseatic League or Hansa	✓	☐
27. Charles Dow	✓	☐
28. King of Rome	✓	☐
29. Ogedei	✗	☐
30. The Spanish Inquisition	✓	☐
SCORE	27/30	___/30

HISTORY POST-1900

THE BEAST

YOU

1. Nuremburg ✓ ☐

> Mark: 'After Manfred von Richthofen (The Red Baron) died and his successor was shot down, Göring took over as the commander of the Jagdgeschwader 1, the elite fighter squadron popularly known as the Jastas or the Flying Circus.'

2. Halley's Comet ✓ ☐
3. Star-Spangled Banner ✓ ☐
4. Apple ✓ ☐
5. Smallpox ✓ ☐
6. Jack Ruby ✓ ☐
7. Insulin ✓ ☐
8. Amelia Earhart ✗ ☐
9. Woodstock ✓ ☐
10. Lockerbie ✓ ☐
11. Anthony Eden ✗ ☐
12. Memphis ✗ ☐
13. First IVF baby ✓ ☐
14. Edith Cavell ✓ ☐
15. Spandau ✓ ☐
16. Luhansk ✓ ☐
17. Mutual Assured Destruction ✓ ☐

	THE BEAST	YOU
18. Portugal	✓	☐

> Mark: 'Portugal is Britain's longest continuous ally. The relationship between the two countries stretches back to the 12th century, when English crusaders helped Alfonso I capture Lisbon from the Moors.'

	THE BEAST	YOU
19. Ferdinand Marcos	✓	☐
20. Dayton	✓	☐
21. W B Yeats	✗	☐
22. Balfour Declaration	✓	☐
23. Liechtenstein	✓	☐
24. Mozambique	✗	☐
25. Bitcoin	✓	☐
26. Mexico	✓	☐
27. Guernica	✓	☐
28. (Operation) Neptune	✓	☐
29. Colin Powell	✓	☐
30. Dorothea Lange	✗	☐
SCORE	24/30	___/30

LITERATURE 1

		THE BEAST	YOU
1.	*Hamlet*	✓	☐
2.	Haiku	✓	☐
3.	*Moby Dick*	✓	☐

> Mark: 'The musician Moby is the great-great nephew of Herman Melville, the author of Moby Dick. Moby's real name is Richard Melville Hall.'

		THE BEAST	YOU
4.	*The Three Sisters*	✓	☐
5.	*The Hitchhiker's Guide to the Galaxy*	✓	☐
6.	John Grisham	✓	☐
7.	*Pandemonium*	✓	☐
8.	*Ulysses*	✓	☐
9.	Nevermore	✓	☐
10.	*Madame Bovary*	✗	☐
11.	Lesbos	✓	☐
12.	Bob Marley	✓	☐
13.	Prometheus	✓	☐
14.	*The Picture of Dorian Gray*	✓	☐
15.	French	✓	☐

> Mark: 'It's one of those weird quirks of circumstance that Samuel Beckett happened to act as a chauffeur for the wrestler André the Giant for a while. They lived in the same French village and a number of adults took turns driving the local kids to school.'

	THE BEAST	YOU
16. Mouse	✓	☐
17. *The Great Gatsby*	✓	☐
18. *Fahrenheit 451*	✓	☐
19. *Anna Karenina*	✗	☐
20. *Orlando*	✓	☐
21. *John Bull's Other Island*	✓	☐
22. Bildungsroman	✗	☐
23. Edith Wharton	✓	☐
24. *Cold Comfort Farm*	✓	☐
25. The goldfinch	✗	☐
26. Grace Metalious	✗	☐
27. *The Girl in the Spider's Web*	✗	☐
28. After Ford	✓	☐
29. *Germinal*	✓	☐
30. Stephen King	✓	☐
SCORE	**24/30**	**___/30**

LITERATURE 2

		THE BEAST	YOU
1.	Anne Boleyn	✓	☐
2.	*Silas Marner*	✓	☐
3.	Fungus	✓	☐
4.	*Nautilus*	✓	☐

> **Mark: 'The USS Nautilus was the world's first nuclear-powered submarine and in 1958 it also became the first submarine to travel under the icecap to the Arctic.'**

		THE BEAST	YOU
5.	Daphne du Maurier	✓	☐
6.	Cured a blind man	✗	☐
7.	*Along Came a Spider*	✓	☐
8.	*A Clockwork Orange*	✓	☐
9.	*The Bell Jar*	✗	☐
10.	*Conversations with Friends*	✗	☐
11.	Oscar Wilde	✓	☐
12.	Charlotte	✗	☐
13.	Amanda Gorman	✗	☐
14.	Iago	✓	☐
15.	Anthony Horowitz	✗	☐
16.	Three (Women)	✗	☐
17.	An author	✓	☐
18.	*The Second Sex*	✗	☐
19.	Asterix	✓	☐

	THE BEAST	YOU
20. Nadine Gordimer	✗	☐
21. *A Visit From the Goon Squad*	✗	☐
22. Artful Dodger	✓	☐
23. Maya Angelou	✓	☐
24. Sikhism	✓	☐
25. Scout	✓	☐
26. *The Great Gatsby*	✓	☐
27. *Swallows and Amazons*	✓	☐

> **Mark: 'Ransome was good friends with the Russian Revolutionary leaders Lenin and Trotsky, often playing chess with them. He even married Trotsky's secretary.'**

	THE BEAST	YOU
28. Thucydides	✗	☐
29. Resurrection Stone	✓	☐
30. Sylvia Plath	✓	☐
SCORE	19/30	___/30

MYTHOLOGY

		THE BEAST	YOU
1.	Jupiter	✓	☐

Mark: *'Jupiter is famously bigger than all the other planets in our solar system put together. One theory suggests that it may even be a failed dwarf star.'*

		THE BEAST	YOU
2.	Camelot	✓	☐
3.	Love	✓	☐
4.	Sherwood Forest	✓	☐
5.	Unicorn	✓	☐
6.	Switzerland	✗	☐
7.	*Argo*	✓	☐
8.	*1,001 Nights* or *Arabian Nights*	✓	☐
9.	Wooden horse	✓	☐

Mark: *'Some historians think that the wooden horse may have been an early version of a siege tower.'*

		THE BEAST	YOU
10.	Banshees	✓	☐

Mark: *'My fellow chaser Anne Hegerty claims she has a family banshee!'*

		THE BEAST	YOU
11.	Rainbow	✓	☐
12.	Poseidon	✗	☐
13.	Hammer	✓	☐

	THE BEAST	YOU
14. Grendel	✓	☐
15. Shoe-makers	✓	☐
16. Tartarus	✗	☐
17. Loch Ness Monster	✓	☐
18. Gemini	✓	☐
19. Cerberus	✓	☐
20. Man	✓	☐
21. Medusa	✓	☐
22. Ragnar Lothbrok	✓	☐
23. Thetis	✗	☐
24. Ask	✗	☐
25. Crete	✓	☐
26. Emperor of Japan	✓	☐

Mark: 'The Japanese monarchy is the oldest continuous hereditary monarchy in the world.'

	THE BEAST	YOU
27. Cat	✗	☐
28. Ixion	✗	☐
29. Romulus	✓	☐
30. Falcon	✓	☐
SCORE	23/30	___/30

PHYSICS

		THE BEAST	YOU
1.	Hertz	✓	☐
2.	Isaac Newton	✓	☐
3.	Nucleus	✓	☐
4.	Kelvin	✓	☐
5.	Speed of light or constant	✓	☐
6.	Doppler effect	✓	☐
7.	Van de Graaf generator	✓	☐
8.	X-rays	✓	☐
9.	(Nuclear) fission	✓	☐
10.	Enrico Fermi	✓	☐
11.	Cation	✓	☐
12.	Refraction	✓	☐
13.	Terminal velocity	✗	☐

Mark: *'Many people consider the cheetah to be the fastest animal on Earth, but the peregrine falcon can reach a terminal velocity of close to 200 mph when it dives for prey.'*

		THE BEAST	YOU
14.	Spin	✗	☐
15.	James Clerk Maxwell	✗	☐
16.	Density	✓	☐
17.	Ballistics	✓	☐
18.	Quark	✓	☐
19.	Black hole	✓	☐

	THE BEAST	YOU
20. Peter Higgs	✓	☐
21. Wolfgang Pauli	✓	☐
22. Gamma rays	✓	☐
23. Parsec	✗	☐

> Mark: 'Perhaps this unit is most famous for Han Solo claiming in *Star Wars* that the Millennium Falcon *did the Kessel Run "in less than 12 parsecs". Unfortunately for Han, a parsec is a unit of distance, not time.'*

	THE BEAST	YOU
24. Torque	✓	☐
25. Max Planck	✓	☐
26. Photoelectric effect	✗	☐
27. Solenoid	✓	☐
28. Entropy	✓	☐
29. Photon	✓	☐
30. Event horizon	✓	☐
SCORE	25/30	___/30

POLITICS

	THE BEAST	YOU
1. George Washington	✓	☐

> *Mark: 'Fidel Castro was a pretty good baseball pitcher. It's rumoured he went to an open tryout for the Washington Senators who were scouting in Havana in the late 1940s.'*

	THE BEAST	YOU
2. Angela Merkel	✓	☐
3. Fidel Castro	✓	☐
4. Hansard	✓	☐
5. Press Secretary	✗	☐
6. James Callaghan	✓	☐

> *Mark: 'James Callaghan is the only person to have held all four of the offices of state: Prime Minister, Chancellor of the Exchequer, Home Secretary, and Foreign Secretary. He was married to his wife for 67 years and died just 11 days after her passing.'*

	THE BEAST	YOU
7. Foggy Bottom	✓	☐
8. Australia	✓	☐
9. Gerald Ford	✓	☐
10. Margaret Thatcher	✓	☐

	THE BEAST	YOU
11. 35	✓	☐

12. Duke of Wellington	✓	☐
13. NATO	✓	☐
14. William Howard Taft	✓	☐
15. Justin Trudeau	✓	☐
16. Arthur Henderson	✗	☐
17. Amazon	✓	☐
18. New Zealand	✓	☐

19. Martin Van Buren	✓	☐
20. Élisabeth Borne	✗	☐
21. Carrie Lam	✓	☐
22. Daniel Ortega	✗	☐
23. Congress	✓	☐
24. Bongbong (also accept BBM)	✗	☐
25. Mary	✓	☐

	THE BEAST	YOU
26. James Garfield	✓	☐
27. California	✓	☐
28. Nagorno-Karabakh	✓	☐
29. Boutros Boutros-Ghali	✗	☐
30. Boris Johnson	✗	☐
SCORE	**23/30**	**___/30**

POP MUSIC PRE-2000

		THE BEAST	YOU
1.	Shaggy	✓	☐
2.	Is this the real life? Is this just fantasy?	✗	☐
3.	Jimi Hendrix	✓	☐
4.	'We Didn't Start the Fire'	✓	☐
5.	Sir Cliff Richard	✓	☐
6.	The Cavern Club	✓	☐
7.	Wet Wet Wet	✓	☐
8.	1970s	✓	☐
9.	1975	✗	☐
10.	The Jam	✓	☐
11.	Games	✓	☐
12.	'Games Without Frontiers'	✓	☐
13.	The Supremes	✓	☐
14.	Sheffield	✗	☐
15.	Kevin	✓	☐
16.	Crush	✓	☐
17.	'You Can't Hurry Love'	✓	☐
18.	Green	✓	☐
19.	*Purple Rain*	✓	☐
20.	David Bowie	✗	☐
21.	Suzi Quatro	✗	☐
22.	Roy Castle	✓	☐

	THE BEAST	YOU
23. France (songs called 'Tour de France' and 'Lost in France')	✓	☐
24. Violins	✓	☐
25. Stevie Wonder	✓	☐
26. Radio Caroline	✓	☐
27. 'Fresh'	✗	☐
28. Mary	✓	☐
29. Hall & Oates	✓	☐
30. S.O.S. Band	✗	☐
SCORE	**23/30**	**___/30**

POP MUSIC POST-2000

		THE BEAST	YOU
1.	Poker	✓	☐
2.	'Someone Like You'	✓	☐
3.	'Mr. Brightside'	✓	☐
4.	Take That	✓	☐
5.	Pompeii	✓	☐
6.	'Running Up That Hill'	✓	☐
7.	Taylor Swift	✓	☐
8.	Eminem	✓	☐
9.	Grime	✓	☐
10.	The White Stripes	✓	☐
11.	LadBaby	✓	☐
12.	Travis Barker	✗	☐
13.	'Viva La Vida'	✓	☐
14.	George Ezra	✓	☐
15.	'Rockstar'	✓	☐
16.	Calvin Harris	✓	☐

> Mark: 'Calvin Harris is very tall, 6ft 5in – almost as tall as me! He is one of those people in a select group of artists that have had ten or more number ones.'

	THE BEAST	YOU
17. Lily Allen	✓	☐

> **Mark: 'Lily Allen is married to David Harbour, who plays Jim Hopper in Stranger Things.'**

	THE BEAST	YOU
18. Lil Nas X	✓	☐
19. 'Mad World'	✓	☐
20. Olivia Rodrigo	✓	☐
21. 'Beggin''	✗	☐
22. Donald Glover	✓	☐
23. +	✓	☐
24. Sandi Thom	✓	☐
25. 'Glamorous'	✗	☐
26. Doja Cat	✗	☐
27. Wet Leg	✗	☐
28. 'Stefania'	✗	☐
29. 'Weird Al' Yankovic	✓	☐
30. The Kid Laroi	✗	☐
SCORE	**23/30**	**___/30**

RELIGION

		THE BEAST	YOU
1.	Damascus	✓	☐
2.	Kippah or yarmulke	✓	☐
3.	Trappist	✓	☐
4.	Dalai Lama	✓	☐
5.	Kaaba	✓	☐
6.	Egypt	✓	☐
7.	Buddha or Siddhārtha Gautama	✓	☐
8.	Gethsemane	✓	☐
9.	Lion	✓	☐
10.	Indonesia	✓	☐
11.	Jordan	✓	☐
12.	Hijab	✓	☐
13.	Fishing	✓	☐
14.	Yom Kippur	✓	☐
15.	Friday	✓	☐
16.	Jainism	✗	☐
17.	Sanskrit	✓	☐
18.	Kabbalah	✓	☐
19.	Wicca	✓	☐
20.	Menorah	✓	☐
21.	Shinto	✓	☐
22.	Unification Church	✓	☐
23.	Bismillah	✓	☐

	THE BEAST	YOU
24. Monkeys	✓	☐
25. Shofar	✗	☐
26. Zoroastrianism	✗	☐
27. (Scallop) shell	✗	☐

Mark: 'Santiago de Compostela is a key part of the plot in Bernard Cornwell's Sharpe's Rifles.'

	THE BEAST	YOU
28. Laozi or Lao Tse	✗	☐
29. Ahimsa	✗	☐
30. Ital	✗	☐
SCORE	**23/30**	**___/30**

SPORT 1

		THE BEAST	YOU
1.	Tour de France	✓	☐
2.	Fishing or angling	✓	☐
3.	State of Origin	✓	☐
4.	Nikola Jokić	✗	☐
5.	Justin Rose	✓	☐
6.	Chilean	✓	☐
7.	Tottenham Hotspur (Spurs)	✓	☐
8.	Yannick Noah	✓	☐

> **Mark: 'His son, Joakim Noah, is – as the question implies – even taller than me at 6ft 11in!'**

		THE BEAST	YOU
9.	Ice hockey	✓	☐
10.	Lawrence Rowe	✗	☐
11.	Christine Ohuruogu	✗	☐
12.	Lyon (also accept Olympique Lyonnais)	✗	☐
13.	John Part	✓	☐
14.	Field hockey	✓	☐
15.	Sergio García	✓	☐
16.	Michael Owen	✓	☐
17.	Bernard Hopkins	✓	☐
18.	Seattle Mariners	✓	☐
19.	Rachael Blackmore	✓	☐
20.	Ten-pin bowling	✓	☐

	THE BEAST	YOU
21. Mosconi Cup	✓	☐
22. 400m hurdles	✓	☐
23. Monaco	✓	☐
24. Basketball	✗	☐
25. Minnesota Vikings	✓	☐
26. Amanda Nunes	✓	☐
27. Gabby Douglas	✗	☐
28. Slovakia	✗	☐
29. Galatasaray	✓	☐
30. Ronnie O'Sullivan	✓	☐
SCORE	**23/30**	**___/30**

SPORT 2

		THE BEAST	YOU
1.	Tiger	✓	☐
2.	Red	✓	☐
3.	50	✓	☐
4.	Usain Bolt	✓	☐
5.	France	✓	☐
6.	Duck	✓	☐
7.	Los Angeles Lakers	✓	☐
8.	Michael Schumacher	✓	☐
9.	Brooklyn	✓	☐

> Mark: 'It was an era-defining moment in baseball when Walter O'Malley moved the team to the West Coast after the 1957 season. Up until then, the game was largely based in the northeastern United States. The New York Giants were also persuaded to move out west and relocated to San Francisco in the same year.'

		THE BEAST	YOU
10.	Milan	✓	☐
11.	Melbourne Cup	✓	☐
12.	Shooting	✓	☐
13.	Submitting	✓	☐

	THE BEAST	YOU
14. Clean and jerk	✓	☐

Mark: 'With the two phases of clean and jerk, you can lift bigger weights. Weightlifting has a unique way of settling a tie by declaring the lightest competitor the winner!'

	THE BEAST	YOU
15. Martina Navratilova	✓	☐
16. Breaststroke	✓	☐
17. Blue	✓	☐
18. Kansas City Chiefs	✓	☐
19. Lake Placid	✓	☐
20. Sonny Liston	✓	☐
21. Indianapolis 500	✓	☐
22. Snake	✓	☐
23. Mr Irrelevant	✗	☐
24. Egypt	✓	☐
25. Table tennis	✓	☐
26. Oslo	✓	☐
27. Julius Irving	✓	☐
28. Yokozuna	✓	☐
29. Arnold Schwarzenegger	✓	☐
30. USA	✓	☐
SCORE	29/30	___/30

SPORT 3

		THE BEAST	YOU
1.	Tyson	✓	☐
2.	Football World Cup	✓	☐
3.	Four	✓	☐
4.	Danny Boyle	✓	☐
5.	Matthew Pinsent	✓	☐
6.	Ossie Ardiles	✓	☐

> *Mark: 'Ossie Ardiles felt that he couldn't play in a country that was at war with his home nation, and the situation was compounded when his cousin was reported missing in action. In 2014, Ardiles travelled to the islands to film a documentary. While there, he had to be airlifted to hospital by the RAF after a car crash.'*

		THE BEAST	YOU
7.	Drop goal	✓	☐
8.	The Curragh	✓	☐
9.	Big Bash	✓	☐
10.	McLaren	✗	☐
11.	From Russia with Love	✓	☐
12.	Seve Ballesteros	✓	☐
13.	Amen Corner	✓	☐
14.	Octagon	✓	☐

	THE BEAST	YOU
15. America's Cup	✗	☐

Mark: 'The cup is named after the yacht that won the first race in 1851. From then until 1983, it was won by American crews, until the Australians beat them to take the competition back to Perth.'

	THE BEAST	YOU
16. Ellen MacArthur	✗	☐
17. Slips	✓	☐
18. Swimming	✓	☐
19. Tiddlywinks	✓	☐
20. *Octopussy*	✓	☐
21. Corsica	✓	☐
22. Basketball	✓	☐
23. Foot and mouth	✓	☐
24. Curling	✓	☐
25. Silverstone	✓	☐
26. Squash	✓	☐
27. Detroit	✓	☐
28. South Africa	✓	☐
29. Chris Eubank	✓	☐
30. Denmark	✗	☐
SCORE	26/30	___/30

TV

		THE BEAST	YOU
1.	USS *Enterprise*	✓	☐
2.	*Baywatch*	✓	☐
3.	Netflix	✓	☐
4.	Lisa	✓	☐
5.	*Game of Thrones*	✓	☐
6.	*The Office*	✓	☐
7.	Korean War	✓	☐

> Mark: 'Prior to streaming services altering the way viewing figures are recorded, the M*A*S*H finale was the most-watched non-sports TV programme on US TV, with over 100 million people tuning in when it was broadcast.'

		THE BEAST	YOU
8.	*Star Wars*	✓	☐
9.	Grantham	✓	☐
10.	Theo (Theodopolus)	✓	☐

> Mark: 'Telly Savalas was Jennifer Aniston's godfather.'

		THE BEAST	YOU
11.	*Battlestar Galactica*	✓	☐
12.	The Fonz	✓	☐
13.	*Band of Brothers*	✓	☐
14.	Melissa Joan Hart	✗	☐
15.	Gunther	✓	☐

	THE BEAST	YOU
16. Werewolf	✓	☐
17. *Beavis and Butt-Head*	✓	☐
18. Sergeant Ernie Bilko	✓	☐
19. Pam Ewing	✓	☐
20. Xena: Warrior Princess	✓	☐
21. Art Fleming	✗	☐
22. The Arrowverse	✗	☐
23. Chameleon circuit	✗	☐
24. Tug of war	✗	☐
25. Denzel Washington	✓	☐
26. Atlanta	✗	☐
27. Augustus	✗	☐
28. BraveStarr	✗	☐
29. The A-Team	✓	☐
30. Gilead	✓	☐
SCORE	22/30	___/30

WORDS & LANGUAGE

		THE BEAST	YOU
1.	Rain	✓	☐
2.	Greek	✓	☐
3.	Tango	✓	☐
4.	Braille	✓	☐

Mark: 'Louis Braille went blind as a child. At the age of 15, he found 63 ways to use a six-dot cell in an area no larger than a fingertip, creating braille as we know it today.'

		THE BEAST	YOU
5.	Mandarin Chinese	✓	☐
6.	22	✓	☐
7.	Hebrew	✓	☐
8.	Bill Bryson	✓	☐
9.	Sanskrit	✓	☐
10.	34	✗	☐
11.	Seize the day	✓	☐
12.	Children, kitchen, church	✗	☐
13.	16th	✓	☐
14.	Semaphore	✗	☐
15.	On holiday	✓	☐
16.	Lord	✗	☐
17.	Computer programming languages or code	✓	☐
18.	Conjunctions	✓	☐
19.	Punjabi	✗	☐

	THE BEAST	YOU
20. 'That's one small step for man. One giant leap for mankind.'	✓	☐
21. An oxymoron	✓	☐
22. Helen Keller	✓	☐
23. Wine (in a box)	✗	☐
24. Infinity	✓	☐
25. Underground	✓	☐
26. The Universal Declaration of Human Rights	✗	☐
27. A tittle	✓	☐
28. Doxing	✗	☐
29. Feedback	✗	☐
30. Rotokas	✗	☐

> *Mark: 'Ah yes! I believe it only has 12 letters.'*

SCORE 20/30 ___/30

AUTHOR'S ACKNOWLEDGEMENTS

I would like to thank David and Sue Hahn,
David Bill at Redtooth and Christian Guiltenane
for making this book possible.

PUBLISHER'S ACKNOWLEDGEMENTS

The Publishers would like to thank David and Sue Hahn
for their hard work and good nature in getting this project
off the ground; David Bill and the team at Redtooth
Quizzes for providing the perfectly pitched questions;
Christian Guiltenane for his industry and skillful writing
under pressure; Mark Harrison for his skill and creativity at
the cover shoot and, last but not least, Mark 'The Beast'
Labbett for maintaining his good humour and keeping us
entertained during the long quizzing sessions.